Budgeting for a Bigger Life

Save Aggressively Without Feeling Like You're Depriving Yourself

Wren Prescott

First edition, 2026

Published by Wren Prescott

Contents

Chapter 1: The Bigger Life Gap	1
Chapter 2: Unearthing Your Core Values	13
Chapter 3: The Values-Based Budget Blueprint	35
Chapter 4: The Flexible Spending Audit	55
Chapter 5: Strategic Cuts Without Sacrifice	71
Chapter 6: Boosting Income for Accelerated Savings	81
Chapter 7: The 'Buffer' & Avoiding Burnout	101
Chapter 8: Tracking Progress & Staying Motivated	121
Chapter 9: Putting It All Together: The 'Future Fund' System	139
Also in the Series	153

Chapter 1: The Bigger Life Gap

I spent eighteen months hitting every savings target I set. Had a color-coded spreadsheet—green for on-track categories, yellow for caution zones, red for anything over budget. Every dollar accounted for. Every latte tracked.

Then my best friend Jenna called.

I was in line at Trader Joe's, staring at a cart full of meal-prepped ingredients I'd calculated to the penny. Jenna's voice was breathless, happy, talking fast the way she does when she's nervous. She was getting married. Beach ceremony in Sayulita, Mexico. Small group—maybe twenty people total. The kind of intimate weekend you remember forever. She wanted me there. Needed me there, actually, because who else was going to keep her from having a meltdown the night before?

I stood there holding a bunch of organic kale I didn't even want, doing math in my head. Flight: probably six hundred, maybe seven. Hotel: three nights, call it four hundred. Meals, drinks, the bachelorette thing, a gift. Easily fifteen hundred dollars. Maybe two thousand.

I had seventeen dollars and forty-three cents in my "Fun Money" category.

I told Jenna I'd check my schedule and get back to her. She knew what that meant. We'd been friends since college. She'd watched me become this person—the one who "checks their schedule" instead of just saying yes to the people they love.

That night I sat at my kitchen table, laptop open, staring at my beautiful, perfectly-optimized budget. And I realized I'd built a system so tight I couldn't say yes to the one thing that actually mattered. I'd optimized myself into a corner.

Here's what nobody tells you about budgeting: the spreadsheet can work perfectly and still fail you completely.

The discipline worked—I hit every target, tracked every expense, never once overdrew my checking account. What failed was the underlying assumption: that financial success meant cutting harder, tracking closer, saying no more often. I'd turned my money into a straightjacket instead of a tool for building the life I wanted.

Sarah Jenkins sits in her Honda Civic outside a Whole Foods in suburban Columbus, Ohio, staring at her phone. It's a Sunday afternoon in October, cold enough that she can see her breath, and she's just calculated—again—how much she and her husband Mark would need for a down payment on that little A-frame cabin they found near Hocking Hills State Park.

Twenty-eight thousand dollars.

They've been talking about it for three years. Every Sunday morning they drive past it on their way back from hiking Old Man's Cave, and Mark says the same thing: "Someday." Sarah used to nod and squeeze his hand. Now she just feels tired. Because "someday" isn't a plan. It's what you say when you don't have a plan.

They aren't broke. Mark's an HVAC technician pulling in around sixty-five thousand a year—good money for southern Ohio. Sarah manages the front office at a dental practice, another forty-two thousand. They have a modest mortgage on a three-bedroom ranch they bought in 2019, one car payment, and a golden retriever named Winston who eats his weight in kibble monthly and has the vet bills to match. On paper, they should be able to save.

But every time they build up a few hundred dollars, something happens.

The furnace quits. Winston eats a sock and needs emergency surgery. Mark's truck throws a check engine light that turns into an eight-hundred-dollar repair. It's not catastrophic. It's just... relentless. And the cabin stays a daydream, the kind of thing they talk about in the abstract but never actually plan for, because planning requires believing it's possible.

Here's what Sarah doesn't see yet: the problem isn't the emergencies.

It's that she and Mark have never built a system that treats the cabin like it's *already* a bill they owe—to their future selves. They save what's left over. And there's never anything left over. Not because they're reckless or bad with money. Because they've structured their entire financial life around *responding* instead of *directing*. Life happens, they react, money flows out, repeat.

Most people live in that gap. Not the gap between rich and poor—the gap between earning enough to get by and actually building toward something that matters. Call it the Bigger Life Gap. It's the distance between your current reality and the experiences you want: the cabin, the sabbatical, the ability to say yes when your best friend gets married on a beach in Mexico.

Discipline doesn't solve a design problem. And the Bigger Life Gap is a design problem.

Most budgets are built like diets: they list what you can't have. No lattes. No subscriptions. No spontaneous Target runs. It's a framework of restriction. And restrictions work for a while—maybe even eighteen months if you're stubborn—but they don't work *toward* anything except the vague virtue of "being good with money."

When Jenna called about her wedding, I didn't have a category for "once-in-a-lifetime experiences with people I love." I had "miscellaneous," and miscellaneous was already spoken for.

You can't budget your way to a bigger life by cutting alone. You need to *design* your spending around what you actually want. Which means knowing what you want in the first place—and most people have never actually stopped to figure that out, not in concrete terms.

Let me show you what a plan looks like.

Ben Cartwright is thirty-eight, works in marketing for a mid-sized tech firm in Austin, and earns ninety-five thousand a year. He's read all the books. He tracks every expense in Mint. He knows exactly where his money goes: ten percent into his 401(k), another eight percent into a high-yield savings account, the rest divided neatly between rent, groceries, utilities, his car lease, and a small entertainment budget. He's doing everything right.

And he's miserable.

Because what Ben actually wants is to take a six-month sabbatical and write the novel he's been outlining in his head for a decade. He has the premise, the main characters, even the opening line. He's been carrying a Moleskine notebook for four years, filling it with scenes and dialogue fragments whenever inspiration hits.

But every time he runs the numbers, it seems impossible. Six months without income? His savings are earmarked: retirement, emergency fund, eventual down payment on a house. There's no room for something as indulgent as a sabbatical.

Except Ben isn't asking for indulgence. He's asking for his life to *mean* something beyond optimized savings rates and efficient grocery shopping. And his budget, for all its precision, has no mechanism for that.

You might be thinking: "Well, sure, but that's just how it works. You save for retirement. You build an emergency fund. You handle the basics first, and *then*, if there's anything left over, you can think about dream stuff like sabbaticals."

That's the conventional wisdom. It's also why most people never close the Bigger Life Gap.

Here's the shift that changes everything: stop thinking of your budget as a list of restrictions and start thinking of it as an *allocation system for your future self*. Not future-future, like retirement-at-sixty-five future. Future as in: the person you'll be in three years. The person you'll be in five years when you want to take that sabbatical. The person you'll be in eighteen months when your best friend gets married and you need to be able to say yes without checking your spreadsheet first.

That version of you—the one living a bigger life—needs funding *now*. And if you wait until you have "extra" money, it'll never happen. Because there's no such thing as extra money. There's only money you've assigned a job to, and money that gets absorbed by the everyday churn of living.

So you have to make the bigger life a bill. A non-negotiable line item, paid first, before Netflix and groceries and the electric company.

"That's easy to say when you have room in your budget. I'm already stretched thin. Where exactly am I supposed to find an extra five hundred dollars a month for some dream fund?"

Fair. Let's talk about that.

Sarah and Mark didn't think they had room either. When I first suggested tracking their spending—not judging it, not restricting it, just *seeing* it—Sarah actually laughed. "I know where our money goes," she said. "It goes to bills and groceries and keeping our lives from falling apart."

But she agreed to try it for sixty days. Just track everything. Every coffee, every grocery run, every automatic subscription charge.

Patterns emerged.

A hundred and sixty dollars a month on takeout—mostly Thai and pizza on weeknights when they were both too exhausted to cook. Sarah works early shifts, Mark works late ones, and by the time they're both home it's eight-thirty and neither of them wants to look at a stove.

Eighty-five dollars on a gym membership neither of them had used in eight months.

Forty dollars on a streaming bundle they'd signed up for during a free trial and forgotten to cancel.

Thirty-something on impulse purchases at Target. You know the drill: you go in for paper towels and come out with throw pillows, a new kitchen gadget, a candle that smells like "eucalyptus mint" and gets lit exactly once.

Another seventy on subscriptions they'd accumulated over time: meal kits they no longer cooked, a wine club that had lost its appeal, premium apps they'd replaced with free alternatives but never bothered to downgrade.

Add it up: three hundred and eighty-five dollars a month, just... leaking out. Not to anything they valued. Not to anything that made their lives better. Just to inertia.

When I asked Sarah which of those expenses she'd genuinely miss if they disappeared tomorrow, she paused. "Maybe the takeout," she said finally. "But honestly, half the time it's not even that good. We just don't want to cook."

So we didn't cut takeout entirely. We cut it in *half*—from twice a week to once a week. Still a relief valve for exhausting days, but more intentional. That freed up eighty dollars.

Canceled the forgotten subscriptions and the unused gym membership: another hundred and fifty-five.

Instituted a forty-eight-hour rule for Target runs: if they saw something they wanted, they'd take a photo of it and wait two days before buying. Ninety percent of the time, the urge passed. That pulled back most of the impulse spending.

Total redirected: three hundred and ten dollars a month.

Not from draconian cuts. Not from eliminating joy or spontaneity. From asking, repeatedly, "Is this getting us closer to the cabin?"

They still needed another hundred and ninety to hit the five hundred they'd calculated for their down payment fund. That meant making more money—something we'll dig into in Chapter 6—but even before they figured that part out, they had *momentum*. For the first time in three years, the cabin wasn't a fantasy. It was a line item. A funded goal. A bill they paid to their future selves every single month.

And here's the thing that surprised Sarah most: she didn't feel deprived.

She felt *relieved*.

Because every dollar they redirected was a dollar that finally had a *purpose*. It wasn't swirling around in vague categories, getting absorbed by life's noise. It was building something they actually wanted. The takeout they still got on Friday nights tasted better because it was a choice they'd made consciously instead of a default setting.

That's the psychological shift most budgeting advice misses. Restriction feels bad. Deprivation feels bad. But *intentionality* feels powerful.

When you're cutting lattes because some finance influencer says lattes are wasteful, you're just punishing yourself. When you're redirecting latte money into your "Lake Cabin Fund" because you'd rather wake up by the water than in line at Starbucks, you're making a choice. You're in control.

Most people feel like their money controls them—bills arrive, they pay them, whatever's left gets spent or saved haphazardly, rinse and repeat. Budgeting for a bigger life flips that. You decide where the money goes *before* life decides for you.

Let me give you a concrete framework for doing that. I call it the Future Fund system. It's simple enough that you can set it up this weekend, and specific enough that it'll actually work when Monday morning chaos hits.

Step one: Name your bigger life.

Not in vague terms. Not "I want financial freedom" or "I want to travel more." In concrete, specific, price-tagged terms.

Sarah and Mark wanted the cabin. Twenty-eight thousand down payment, five-year timeline.

Ben wanted his sabbatical. Eighteen thousand to cover six months of living expenses, three-year timeline.

I wanted to be able to say yes to things like Jenna's wedding without a panic attack—so I needed a "Life Happens Fund" with at least five thousand in it, built over twelve months.

Your turn. What do you want your money to *do* for you in the next one to five years?

Write it down. Get specific. If it's a trip, where? When? How much will flights cost? Hotels? If it's a career break, how long? What are your monthly expenses during that time? If it's starting a business, what are the actual startup costs?

Don't worry about whether it seems realistic yet. Just get it on paper. You need a target before you can design a path to hit it.

If you're drawing a blank—if you've been in survival mode so long that dreaming feels foreign—try this: think about the last time you felt genuinely envious of someone. Not resentful. Not bitter. Just that clean, sharp pang of "I wish I could do that." What were they doing? That's your clue.

Step two: Reverse-engineer the monthly number.

Take the total cost and divide it by the number of months until you need it. That's your monthly funding target.

Sarah and Mark needed five hundred a month for the cabin. Ben needed five hundred a month for his sabbatical. I needed four hundred and seventeen a month for my Life Happens Fund—which I rounded up to four-fifty to give myself a buffer.

If that number makes you laugh out loud because there's no possible way you have that much room in your budget, stay with me.

Step three: Find the money that's already leaving.

This is where most people discover they have more control than they thought.

Track your spending for thirty days. Not to judge yourself. Not to feel guilty. Just to *see*. You're looking for patterns:

- Subscriptions you forgot about or no longer use - Habits that aren't serving you (daily takeout, unused memberships, impulse purchases) - "Lifestyle creep" expenses—things you started buying when you got a raise that are now just part of the baseline

Sarah and Mark found three hundred and ten a month this way. You might find more. You might find less. But you'll almost certainly find *something*.

The average American household has at least four forgotten subscription services. Four. That's probably a hundred to two hundred dollars a month, just evaporating.

Step four: Bridge the gap.

If step three doesn't get you all the way to your monthly funding target, you have two options: extend your timeline (if the cabin takes seven years instead of five, the monthly number drops to around three-thirty), or increase your income (side hustle, negotiating a raise, selling stuff you don't need).

We'll tackle income strategies in Chapter 6. For now, just know that you're not trapped. You have levers. If you can't pull the spending lever far enough, you can pull the income lever. Or the timeline lever.

Step five: Automate the transfer.

This is the part that makes it actually happen instead of just being a nice idea you forget about by February.

Open a separate savings account—could be at your current bank, could be a high-yield account at an online bank like Ally or Marcus—and name it after your goal. "Cabin Fund." "Sabbatical Fund." "Life Happens Fund." Then set up an automatic transfer from your checking account on the day after you get paid. Every paycheck, before you pay rent or buy groceries or do anything else, that money moves into the fund.

It's not willpower. It's infrastructure.

Treat it like you treat your electric bill. You don't sit around every month deciding whether you *feel* like paying the power company. The money just goes. Same with your Future Fund. You're paying a bill to the future version of yourself who gets to live a bigger life because present-you designed it that way.

Maria Gonzalez is a single mom in Albuquerque. She's a night-shift nurse pulling in about sixty-two thousand a year after overtime—good money, but not "coasting" money, especially as a single parent. Her daughter Sofia is seven, obsessed with science documentaries and marine biology, the kind of kid who asks questions that require googling to answer.

Maria's bigger life goal is simple: she wants Sofia to go to college without drowning in debt.

She's seen too many young nurses start their careers already fifty thousand in the hole, working extra shifts just to stay current on loan payments, delaying buying a house or starting a family or doing anything except servicing debt.

Jenna was calling about Iceland. Ten days, late September, northern lights. She'd found cheap flights. I looked at my spreadsheet. I said no.

The spreadsheet was perfect. The priorities weren't.

Chapter 2: Unearthing Your Core Values

I watched my friend Rachel cry in a Target parking lot at 2 PM on a Wednesday. Not the quiet, dignified kind of crying. The gasping, mascara-running kind that makes strangers look away.

Not the quiet, dignified kind of crying. The gasping, mascara-running kind that makes strangers look away. She'd just spent $340 on things she couldn't even remember picking up—throw pillows, candles, a decorative ladder (a *ladder*)—and her daughter's dance recital costume, the one she'd promised to buy weeks ago, was still sitting in the cart. Unpurchased. Because after the impulse spree, she didn't have enough left on her debit card.

"I don't know what's wrong with me," she kept saying. "I *know* better. I *know* I should save. I know Emma's costume matters more than... whatever the hell this is." She gestured at the bags in her trunk like they contained evidence of a crime.

Here's what I didn't say, because it would have been useless in that moment: Nothing was wrong with her.

Rachel's problem wasn't discipline. It wasn't willpower. It wasn't even that she was "bad with money."

Her problem was that she had no idea what she actually valued.

And before you roll your eyes—I know, I *know* this sounds like the kind of thing a wellness influencer says before selling you a $47 PDF—hear me out. Because what I'm talking about isn't some ethereal journey to discover your "authentic self." I'm talking about the brutally practical work of figuring out where your money should actually go if you want to stop feeling like Rachel in that parking lot.

Most of us are walking around with a vague sense that we *should* want certain things. Financial security, obviously. A nice home. Maybe travel, if we're the "adventurous type." We absorb these priorities from parents, from social media, from the fact that everyone at work seems to be renovating their kitchen or planning a trip to Europe. And then we spend our money trying to chase all of it at once, spreading ourselves so thin that nothing gets the resources it actually needs to matter.

The result?

You're perpetually broke, perpetually behind, and perpetually confused about why you feel so empty despite "treating yourself" constantly.

I know what you're thinking: "Great, another lecture about how I should value experiences over things, right? How I should be grateful and mindful and blah blah blah?"

No. That's not what this is.

This is about getting so honest with yourself that it's uncomfortable. It's about recognizing that you *cannot* prioritize everything, and that the act of trying to do so is exactly what's keeping you stuck. Some things matter more than others. Some things deserve your money and attention. And a whole lot of things you're currently spending on? They're just noise.

Let me tell you what it costs to keep living without this clarity. Not in some abstract, "you'll regret it someday" sense. I mean right now. Today.

You know that feeling when you check your bank account and feel a little sick, even though you're technically "fine"? That low-grade anxiety that hums in the background of every transaction? That's the cost. You're spending money, but you don't know if it's on the right things, so every purchase carries this tiny weight of doubt. *Did I need this? Should I have bought that? Am I screwing up my future by getting coffee today?*

Or maybe you're the type who avoids looking at your account altogether. You swipe your card and hope for the best, and the not-knowing becomes its own kind of tax. You can't relax because you're never quite sure if you're okay or if you're one unexpected expense away from disaster.

And then there's the stuff you accumulate.

The things you bought because they were on sale, or because everyone else had one, or because you thought they'd make you happy. They're piled in your closet, shoved in drawers, cluttering your counters. You look at them and feel... nothing. Or worse, you feel guilt. Because you spent money on them. Money you now wish you had for something else. Something you can't quite name, but you know it would have mattered more.

That's the cost of not knowing your values. It's not some distant consequence. It's the daily, grinding sensation that your money is leaking away into a void, and you have no idea how to stop it.

Here's the thing I wish someone had told me fifteen years ago, when I was making decent money and still felt like I was drowning: your budget will never work if it's built on someone else's priorities.

I spent *years*—and I mean actual years, not just a few frustrating months—trying to follow advice from personal finance gurus who had their lives perfectly mapped out. They knew exactly what they valued. Their spreadsheets had purpose. Meanwhile, I was over here funding a 401(k) (because that's what responsible adults do), saving for a house down payment (because homeownership is the dream, right?), and occasionally panic-buying expensive workout equipment I'd use twice before it became a very expensive clothes hanger.

None of it felt like *mine*. It felt like I was living someone else's script.

I'd get my paycheck, pay my bills, and then watch the rest evaporate on things I barely remembered buying. I'd occasionally panic and try to "get serious" about budgeting, downloading apps and tracking every transaction for about nine days before giving up because it felt pointless. The numbers didn't *mean* anything.

What changed wasn't that I suddenly developed superhuman willpower. What changed was that I got honest—really, painfully honest—about what I actually cared about. And I stopped pretending that I cared about things I didn't.

Here's the exercise that did it. I call it the Values Sort, and it's deceptively simple. You're going to write down ten life areas—just write them in a list, don't think too hard about it:

Health Relationships (family & friends) Career/Work Personal Growth Experiences (travel, hobbies) Financial Security Community Involvement Creativity Spirituality Physical Environment (home, location)

Now rank them. One through ten. Most important to least.

And here's where people get stuck: they start trying to rank them based on what they *should* value. What a "good person" would prioritize. What their parents would approve of. What sounds impressive.

Stop.

This isn't for anyone else. If you rank "Experiences" at the top and "Community Involvement" at the bottom, that doesn't make you selfish. It makes you honest. And honesty is the only thing that's going to help you here.

When I did this exercise myself, "Financial Security" ended up at number seven. *Seven*. This shocked me, because I spent an enormous amount of mental energy worrying about money. But when I really thought about it? I didn't actually value financial security for its own sake. I valued what I thought it would give me: freedom to take creative risks, time with people I loved, the ability to say no to work I hated.

Those things—creativity, relationships, autonomy—those were the actual values. Financial security was just a tool. A means to an end.

Once I saw that, everything shifted. I stopped treating "save more money" as the goal and started asking: What am I saving *for*? What do I actually want this money to *do*?

You might find something similar when you do this. Or you might discover that financial security genuinely is your top priority—not because you "should" value it, but because the feeling of stability and safety is what allows you to breathe. That's valid too. The point isn't to arrive at the "right" ranking. The point is to know *your* ranking.

Let me show you what this looks like in practice.

Mark was a guy I worked with a few years ago—mid-thirties, steady job, chronically broke despite earning a solid income. When we sat down and looked at where his money was going, almost all of his discretionary spending was on electronics and collectibles. Limited-edition sneakers. Vintage video games. The latest phone, the newest headphones, the upgraded version of something he already owned.

I asked him to do the Values Sort. He resisted at first—thought it was touchy-feely nonsense—but eventually he humored me. His top two values? "Personal Growth" and "Experiences."

He stared at the list for a long time. Then he said, "I don't spend any money on this."

He didn't. Not a dollar. No classes, no books, no trips. His entire budget was going toward things that—when he was really honest—he didn't care about that much. He *liked* the sneakers. He enjoyed the hunt for rare games. But he didn't *value* them. Not in the way he valued learning and adventure.

"So why do I keep buying this stuff?" he asked.

Good question. And the answer, I think, is that it's easier. Easier to click "buy now" on something tangible than to plan a trip or research a course or commit to learning a new skill. Easier to fill the void with *something* than to sit with the discomfort of realizing you're not living the life you actually want.

Once Mark saw the disconnect, he started making different choices. Not perfect choices—he didn't suddenly become a monk—but *different* ones. He set up a dedicated fund for travel and online courses. He unsubscribed from the marketing emails that fed his impulse buying. He sold some of the collectibles he'd been hoarding and barely looked at.

Six months later, he'd taken a weekend trip to Montreal (something he'd been "planning" for years) and enrolled in a French class. He seemed lighter. Less cluttered, both physically and mentally.

That's what happens when your spending aligns with your values. It's not about deprivation. It's about directing your resources toward things that actually fill you up instead of letting them scatter across things that don't.

Now—you're probably thinking, "Okay, fine, but how does this translate into actual budgeting? I still have bills to pay and a finite amount of money."

Right. And that's exactly where this gets practical.

Your values become your filter. Instead of asking "Can I afford this?" every time you're tempted to buy something, you ask: "Does this align with my top three priorities?"

If the answer is no, that doesn't mean you can never buy it. But it does mean you pause. You consider. You make a *choice* rather than operating on autopilot.

Think of your budget as a value statement written in dollars. Every purchase is a vote for what matters to you. If you say you value health, but your budget shows daily fast food and zero money for fresh groceries or a gym membership, there's a disconnect. If you say you value relationships, but you never set aside money for quality time with loved ones—dinners, trips, gifts, whatever strengthens those bonds—then your budget is lying.

And budgets don't lie. They just reflect reality.

Let me walk you through another example, because I think this is where the concept really clicks.

Lisa is a teacher. She's 29. She dreams about taking a year off to travel through Southeast Asia—Thailand, Vietnam, Cambodia, the whole route. She's been dreaming about this for five years. When she did the Values Sort, "Experiences" and "Personal Growth" landed at the top, followed by "Financial Security."

But she wasn't saving for the trip.

She was stuck in a loop where every month she'd set aside a little money, and then something would come up—drinks with coworkers, a new dress, a subscription she forgot to cancel—and the savings would evaporate.

When we dug into her spending, we found she was hemorrhaging about $400 a month on things that didn't connect to any of her values. Daily lattes (not because she loved coffee, but because it was part of her morning routine). Online shopping binges (usually late at night when she was tired and bored). Frequent restaurant meals (mostly out of convenience, not enjoyment).

None of these things were *bad*. But they weren't contributing to her top priorities. They were just... there. Filling space. Filling time.

Here's what she did: She started making coffee at home—not fancy pour-over stuff, just decent coffee in a regular pot. She unsubscribed from every marketing email (this one turned out to be huge). She meal-prepped on Sundays so she wasn't constantly grabbing takeout. And she implemented the 24-hour rule: before buying anything non-essential, she waited a full day. If she still wanted it after 24 hours, fine. But most of the time, the urge had passed.

These changes freed up about $350 a month. Not life-changing money. But money she could *direct*. She funneled $200 into her Southeast Asia fund. She put $100 toward retirement (because "Financial Security" did rank in her top three, and ignoring it completely would have stressed her out). And she kept $50 for genuinely meaningful splurges—concerts, books, meals with friends who mattered.

The shift wasn't in how much money she had. The shift was in the *intention* behind where it went. She stopped passively letting her money disappear and started actively investing it in the life she wanted to create.

This is what I mean when I say budgeting isn't about restriction. It's about allocation. It's about making sure your money works *for* you instead of against you.

I know this can feel overwhelming. You might be looking at your current spending and thinking, "But I like my daily coffee. I don't want to give up everything that brings me joy."

You're not supposed to. That's not the point.

The point is to distinguish between things that bring you fleeting pleasure and things that create lasting fulfillment. Between things you do out of habit and things you do out of genuine desire. Between things that align with your core values and things that... don't.

Some expenses won't neatly fit into a "value" category, and that's fine. You still need car insurance. You still need to pay rent. Nobody's asking you to assign a deep existential meaning to your utility bill. Those are just the realities of modern life. This exercise isn't about guilt. It's about *conscious allocation*.

And some things will fall lower on your list—that's okay too. It has to be. You can't prioritize everything, remember? If "Community Involvement" ranks at number nine for you, that doesn't make you a bad person. It just means that when you're deciding how to spend your Saturday afternoon, you're going to choose the thing that aligns with your higher-ranked values. Maybe that's spending time with family (Relationships) or going for a long hike (Health, or maybe Experiences). That's not selfishness. That's clarity.

Think of it like this: You have ten units of energy each day. Three of them *have* to go toward essential maintenance—commuting, basic hygiene, preparing food. That leaves seven for everything else. Would you spread those seven evenly across all your priorities, giving each one a tiny sliver of your attention? Or would you concentrate five of them on the one or two things that genuinely fuel you, knowing that the others might get less?

Most people, if they think about it honestly, would choose concentration.

Money works the same way.

Here's what often happens when people start this process: they panic. They worry that identifying their values means they have to eliminate everything else. That if travel is their top priority, they can never eat at a nice restaurant again. That if financial security ranks high, they're doomed to a joyless existence of rice and beans.

That's not how this works.

Sarah—Rachel's sister, actually—had the same fear. She loved trying new restaurants, going to concerts, taking spontaneous weekend trips. When we started talking about values, she got anxious. She thought I was going to tell her to stop having fun.

But when we dug deeper, she admitted something: those activities didn't actually fill her up the way she thought they would. They were fun in the moment, sure. But afterwards? She felt kind of empty. And definitely broke.

What *did* fill her up—what genuinely energized her and made her feel like herself—was volunteering at an animal shelter, taking pottery classes, and spending real, quality time with close friends. Not group outings or loud events. Actual conversation. Connection.

And those things cost significantly less.

She wasn't giving up fun. She was redirecting her resources toward things that created genuine fulfillment instead of fleeting gratification. It's a subtle shift, but it changes everything.

So how do you actually unearth these values? Because I know a lot of people struggle with this. They're so caught up in the daily grind, in what they "should" want, in keeping up with what everyone else is doing, that they've lost touch with what they actually care about.

Here's a framework that works. Grab a piece of paper—actual paper, not your phone, because writing by hand forces you to slow down—and divide it into four quadrants. Label them: Relationships, Growth, Experiences, Security.

Set a timer for five minutes per quadrant, and just brainstorm. Write down everything that comes to mind, no matter how small or silly it seems. Don't censor yourself. Don't worry about whether it "makes sense." Just write.

Under "Relationships," think about the people who matter most. What activities do you love doing with them? How do you like to show appreciation?

Under "Growth," consider what skills or knowledge you want to develop. What are you curious about? What have you always wanted to learn?

"Experiences" covers the adventures and memories you crave—travel, sure, but also smaller things. Nature. Music. Food. Whatever lights you up.

And "Security" is about what makes you feel stable and safe. Financial freedom, yes, but maybe also health, or a comfortable home, or knowing you have an emergency fund.

Once you've filled in all four quadrants, step back. Look for patterns. Which categories have the longest lists? Which items feel the most urgent, the most true?

You might discover that "Growth" dominates—that you have a deep drive to keep learning and evolving. Or maybe "Relationships" takes up the most space, revealing that connection and belonging matter more to you than anything else.

Don't overthink it. Trust your gut. This isn't a personality quiz. This is about uncovering the principles that *should* be guiding your decisions—and your budget—if you want to build a life that actually feels like yours.

Now, refine those values into specific statements. Not "I value relationships," but "I want to prioritize deep, meaningful connection with my family and closest friends through regular quality time." Not just "growth," but "I want to continuously expand my skills and knowledge so I can do work that feels fulfilling."

The more specific you are, the easier it becomes to align your budget.

David, a software engineer I know, initially said his top value was "security." But when we pushed deeper, he realized security wasn't about hoarding money. It was about making sure his kids had access to good education and opportunities. His refined statement became: "Providing my children with the resources and support they need to build meaningful lives."

That one shift changed everything. He started prioritizing college savings over expensive vacations—not because vacations were "bad," but because they didn't align with what he actually valued most. And he didn't feel deprived. He felt focused.

You can also rank your values *within* each quadrant if you want to get really granular. If "spending quality time with family" matters more to you than "maintaining a wide social circle," give it a higher weight. This helps when you're making tough choices and resources are limited.

And look—these values aren't set in stone. They'll evolve as your life changes. What matters most in your twenties might look completely different from what matters in your fifties. That's normal. That's human. The key is to revisit this exercise regularly—maybe once a year—to make sure your budget still reflects where you actually are, not where you were five years ago.

I revisit mine every January. And every year, something shifts slightly. Some years, financial security climbs higher because I'm dealing with uncertainty at work. Other years, creativity surges to the top because I'm feeling stagnant. The budget adjusts accordingly. It's not rigid. It's *responsive*.

That's the whole point. You're not locking yourself into some unchangeable system. You're creating a framework that adapts to your life while keeping you anchored to what matters.

Let's get concrete for a second. Say your fixed expenses—rent, utilities, car payment, insurance—total $2,500 a month. After those are covered, you have $1,200 left. This is your discretionary money, and here's where most people go wrong: they treat it like it's all the same. Like every dollar has equal weight.

But if you've done the work above, you know that's not true. Some of those dollars should go toward your top-ranked values. Some toward your middle-tier priorities. And some—honestly, not much—toward things that rank low but still bring you a little joy.

Here's a simple allocation model that works for most people:

60% to your top three values. That's $720. This is where the bulk of your discretionary spending goes. If "Experiences" ranks high, this might be your travel fund, your concert tickets, your weekend adventures. If "Health" is at the top, this is your gym membership, your meal prep ingredients, maybe a therapy copay. If "Personal Growth" dominates, this is books, courses, workshops, coaching.

25% to middle-tier values. That's $300. These are things you care about but not as intensely. Maybe you ranked "Community Involvement" at number six, so you donate a bit each month or occasionally volunteer at events that require registration fees. Or "Physical Environment" landed in the middle, so you set aside money for small home improvements that make your space more comfortable.

15% for everything else. That's $180. This is your guilt-free spending on things that don't align with your values at all but still bring you a little happiness. A nice dinner out just because. A spontaneous purchase that makes you smile. You're not a robot. You don't have to optimize every single dollar. But notice how small this category is compared to the others. That's intentional.

This isn't a perfect formula—nothing is—but it's a starting point. You can adjust the percentages based on your own life. Maybe you want 70% going to your top values and only 10% to miscellaneous stuff. Fine. The key is that you're making a *choice* rather than letting your money wander off without direction.

And here's the part that surprised me when I started doing this: it actually feels *less* restrictive than not having a plan. Because when you know exactly how much you've allocated to, say, dining out, you can enjoy that meal without guilt. You're not wondering if you "should" be saving this money instead. You already *are* saving—for the things that matter more. This meal is accounted for. It's part of the plan.

Compare that to the old way, where every purchase came with a vague sense of unease because you had no idea if you were overspending or underspending or completely screwing up your future. That's exhausting. This is liberating.

I'm not saying it's easy. Especially at first. You're going to mess up. You're going to have months where you blow past your "everything else" budget because you got stressed and online-shopped your feelings. You're going to have moments where you resent the system and wish you could just spend without thinking.

That's normal. The difference is that now, when you mess up, you know exactly *what* you're messing up. You're not just vaguely feeling bad about money. You're seeing a specific misalignment between your values and your choices. And that clarity makes it so much easier to course-correct.

When I overspend on something that doesn't align with my values, I don't spiral into shame. I just acknowledge it. "Okay, I spent $200 on clothes I don't need because I was bored. That money was supposed to go toward my creative projects fund. Next month, I'm going to redirect $200 from my 'everything else' category to make up for it." Done. No drama.

This is where a lot of traditional budgeting advice falls apart. It treats every deviation from the plan as a moral failure. You went over budget? You lack discipline. You didn't stick to your spending limits? You're weak.

Bullshit.

You're human. You're going to make imperfect choices. The system I'm describing doesn't demand perfection. It demands *awareness*. As long as you know what you value and you're generally moving money in that direction, you're doing fine.

Let me tell you about one more person, because I think her story illustrates something important.

Jenny was in her early forties when we met. Divorced, two teenage kids, working full-time in a job she tolerated but didn't love. When she did the Values Sort, "Relationships" and "Personal Growth" topped her list. But her budget told a different story.

She was spending hundreds of dollars a month on her ex-husband's hobbies—because she still felt guilty about the divorce. She was paying for streaming services she never watched, gym memberships she never used, subscriptions she'd forgotten existed. And she was chronically stressed about money, even though her income was solid.

The issue wasn't income. The issue was that her spending had no connection to what she actually cared about.

When we laid out her values next to her actual expenses, the disconnect was stark. She wasn't investing in her relationships—no money set aside for quality time with her kids, no budget for maintaining friendships. She wasn't investing in her growth—no courses, no books, no coaching, nothing that would help her figure out what she actually wanted to do with her life.

She was just... paying for things. Passively. Out of habit or guilt or inertia.

The first step was brutal: she canceled everything that didn't align with her top three values. All of it. The streaming services, the unused memberships, the guilt-driven expenses for her ex. It felt harsh. She worried she was being selfish.

But within two months, she had an extra $400 a month. And for the first time in years, she could breathe.

She used some of that money to take her kids on small adventures—nothing extravagant, just day trips and experiences they could share. She used some to enroll in a weekend workshop on career transitions. And she put the rest into a "future fund" for things she hadn't figured out yet but knew she wanted.

The shift in her demeanor was visible. She stopped looking so worn down. She started talking about possibilities instead of obligations.

That's what this work does. It doesn't just change your budget. It changes how you feel about your life.

Because here's the truth: when your money aligns with your values, you stop feeling like you're constantly sacrificing. You stop feeling like you're choosing between "being responsible" and "having a life." You're just... living. Making choices that reflect who you are and what you care about.

And the people around you notice. Your kids notice when you're less stressed about money. Your partner notices when you stop impulse-buying things you don't need. Your friends notice when you start showing up differently—more present, more intentional, more *you*.

This isn't just about money. It's about reclaiming your life from the default settings society handed you. From the idea that you have to want what everyone else wants. From the belief that discipline and deprivation are the only paths to financial stability.

You don't need more willpower. You need a system that actually reflects your priorities. You need a budget that feels like *yours*.

So here's what I want you to do. Right now, before you move on to the next chapter or get distracted by something else: grab that piece of paper. Draw those four quadrants. Set a timer. Start writing.

Don't overthink it. Don't worry about getting it "right." Just get honest with yourself about what actually matters.

Because until you do, every budget you build is going to feel like someone else's plan. And someone else's plan is never going to work for you.

When you actually sit down and do that exercise—really do it, not just read past it—something interesting happens. The first few things you write down are usually the "right" answers. The ones you're supposed to say. Family. Health. Security. Freedom.

All true. All important. But also… surface level.

It's when you keep going, when you push past the obvious answers and start writing the stuff that feels a little uncomfortable to admit, that you get somewhere useful. That's when you might write down things like: "I want people to think I'm successful." Or "I don't want to feel behind anymore." Or "I'm tired of saying no to things I actually want."

Those aren't Instagram caption values. They're real. And they're *useful*, because they explain behavior in a way that "family" and "security" don't.

Here's what I mean. Let's say you keep upgrading your phone every year even though your current one works fine. If you ask yourself why, the surface answer might be "because I value technology" or "because I need it for work." But if you're honest—if you dig into that quadrant where you're spending money without joy—you might realize it's actually about not wanting to feel left behind. About keeping up. About the fear that being a generation behind on anything signals that you're falling behind in general.

That's not a character flaw. That's just a value you haven't named yet. And once you name it, you can decide what to do with it. You can decide if "not feeling left behind" is worth $1,200 a year. You can decide if there are cheaper ways to meet that need. Or you can decide it *is* worth it, and stop feeling guilty about it, and cut something else instead.

But you can't make any of those decisions until you're honest about what's actually driving the behavior.

The same thing happens in the quadrant where you're *not* spending money but wish you were. That one tends to surprise people. Because it's not about what you can't afford—it's about what you're not letting yourself have, even when you could.

Maybe it's the art class you keep putting off because it feels frivolous. Maybe it's the nicer coffee beans, or the house cleaner, or the trip to visit your best friend. Things that would genuinely make your life better, but you've internalized some story about how "responsible people" don't spend money on that. How you don't "deserve" it yet. How it's wasteful or selfish or indulgent.

Except here's the thing: if you value creativity, and you're not letting yourself take the art class, your budget isn't aligned with your values. It's aligned with someone else's idea of responsibility. If you value rest, and you're burning yourself out because hiring help feels like cheating, you're not being responsible. You're just being stubborn.

This is where people get stuck. They build budgets that are technically sound—every dollar accounted for, savings on track, debt shrinking—but they're miserable. Because the budget is built on *other people's* values. On what's "supposed to" matter, not what actually does.

And then they wonder why they can't stick to it. Why they keep breaking their own rules. Why willpower keeps failing them.

It's not failing. It's just that your actual priorities keep asserting themselves, and you keep trying to override them with discipline instead of just… listening.

So look at what you wrote in those quadrants. Look at the gaps. The contradictions. The stuff that doesn't match the story you tell yourself about who you are.

If you say you value health but you're not spending money on decent food or a gym membership or the physical therapy you've been putting off—what's that about? Is it really that you can't afford it? Or is there another value competing? Maybe you value security more, and spending money on anything that isn't strictly necessary feels too risky. Maybe you value independence, and asking for help or investing in support feels like admitting weakness.

Neither of those is wrong. But if you don't know that's what's happening, you'll just keep beating yourself up for "not prioritizing your health," when the real issue is that you haven't figured out how to honor both values at once.

That's what this chapter is actually about. Not making a list of nice-sounding words. But excavating the real, messy, contradictory priorities that are already running your financial life—whether you've named them or not.

Because here's the truth: you already have a budget. It's just an unconscious one. Every time you swipe your card, every time you say yes or no to something, you're making a decision about what matters. You're allocating resources. You're building a spending pattern.

The question isn't whether you have priorities. The question is whether you've looked at them clearly enough to decide if they're actually *yours*. Or if you're still running someone else's script. Your parents' script about what "financial responsibility" looks like. Your friends' script about what you're supposed to spend money on at this stage of life. The internet's script about hustle and sacrifice and delaying gratification until some distant future when you'll finally have "enough."

Most people never ask that question. They just keep trying to force themselves into budgets that don't fit. They keep wondering why it's so hard. Why everyone else seems to have it figured out.

But the people who actually have it figured out? They're not following someone else's plan. They're building their own. And that starts here. With honesty. With naming what actually matters, not what's supposed to matter.

So go back to that piece of paper. Look at what you wrote. Sit with it. Let yourself be uncomfortable with the gaps, the contradictions, the stuff that doesn't sound as noble as you'd like.

Because that's where the real work begins.

The dance costume was $47. Less than the decorative ladder Rachel couldn't explain buying. Her daughter wore it once, for a five-minute recital, then never again. Rachel still has the photo from that night on her desk.

Rachel knew, sitting in that parking lot, what mattered. She just didn't have a budget that knew it too.

Chapter 3: The Values-Based Budget Blueprint

When was the last time you looked at your bank statement and felt like it was actually yours? Not just accurate - yours. A document that reflected the life you're trying to build, not just the life you happened to live last month.

Tom makes decent money. Around $65,000 a year as a project manager at a healthcare company. He's been talking about buying a house since 2019—back when that seemed difficult but possible, before the market went completely insane. "I just don't know where it goes," he said, scrolling through transaction after transaction on his phone. Starbucks. Amazon. DoorDash. Netflix, Hulu, Disney+, HBO Max. A new pair of running shoes he'd worn exactly twice. None of it bad. None of it wrong. Just... there. Unremarkable. The financial equivalent of empty calories.

The math was simple and brutal: at $47 in savings after six years of actively wanting to buy a house, he was roughly 1,277 years away from a down payment.

Tom isn't lazy. I need you to understand that. He isn't irresponsible or careless with money. He doesn't blow his paycheck on poker or luxury watches. He's just caught in the same trap most people accept as completely normal: the pay-what's-left model. You cover the essentials—rent, utilities, car payment, insurance, all the stuff that hits automatically—and then you live your life with whatever remains. And if there's anything left after living? Sure, maybe you save it. Maybe.

Except there's never anything left.

Here's what nobody tells you about the pay-what's-left approach, and this is the part that makes me genuinely angry: it doesn't just fail to build wealth. It actively prevents you from ever becoming the person who *could* build wealth. Because every month that passes with nothing saved isn't just a missed opportunity. It's confirmation of a story you're telling yourself about who you are. *I'm not a saver. I'm not the disciplined type. I don't have enough.*

And the cruelest part? You're working just as hard as someone who's steadily building toward their dream. You're making sacrifices. You're saying no to things, skipping purchases, feeling guilty about spending. But it's all reactive. All damage control. You're playing defense with your own life, and defense doesn't score points.

I know what you're thinking. *Easy to criticize from wherever you're sitting, but rent is rent. Bills are bills. There's genuinely nothing left.* And I'm not dismissing that—I've been broke enough times to know that sometimes the math is legitimately impossible. But here's the uncomfortable question I need you to sit with: how much of your spending is truly essential versus just... habitual? Automatic? The path of least resistance?

Because here's what I've seen happen over and over, and I bet you've seen it too: people who swear they have absolutely no room to save somehow find money when something matters enough. When their kid needs braces. When the car dies and they can't get to work without it. When their sister's getting married in Maui and they absolutely cannot miss it. When their dog needs emergency surgery. Suddenly, money materializes. Not because they earned more that month—because the priority shifted. Because "I can't afford it" turned into "I have no choice."

The system I'm about to show you isn't some revolutionary concept I invented in a moment of genius. It's just taking that emergency-mode clarity—that thing that happens when you *have* to find the money—and making it permanent. It's deciding, right now, today, that your bigger life isn't less important than your sister's wedding. That your dream of opening a bookstore or retiring early or spending a year traveling through Southeast Asia deserves the same urgency you'd give to replacing a broken transmission.

Here's the shift, and it's simple enough that you might think it can't possibly work: you treat savings for your biggest life goal as a non-negotiable expense.

Not as a nice-to-have. Not as what-you'll-do-if-there's-extra. As a bill you *must* pay, the same exact way you pay rent.

Think about how you approach rent. You don't assess your bank account mid-month and think, *Hmm, do I feel like paying rent this time? Am I in the mood?* You don't pay half because you found a great deal on concert tickets and the show's only in town one night. Rent is sacred. It happens. The money has to be there because the alternative—eviction, your stuff on the sidewalk, scrambling to find somewhere to sleep—is completely unacceptable.

Now imagine treating your future with that same severity.

The mechanics are almost stupidly simple, which is why most people dismiss them. First, you get specific about what you're actually saving for. Not "financial freedom" or "security" or any of those vague concepts that sound important but don't mean anything concrete enough to guide actual decisions. I mean specific enough to visualize. Like: *a down payment of $45,000 for a two-bedroom condo in that neighborhood in Austin near the park by November 2029.* Or: *$380,000 in retirement savings so I can quit my job at 58 instead of working until I'm too old to enjoy it.* Or: *$18,000 to spend six months in Spain learning ceramics without having to work, staying in that small town I read about.*

The specificity matters more than you think because vague goals don't survive contact with a sale at Target. "Financial freedom" loses to "these throw pillows would really tie the room together" every single time. But "quit my job in twelve years"? That's a fight worth having. That's a real trade-off you can weigh in the moment.

Once you know the target—and I mean really know it, can picture it, can describe what it'll feel like when it happens—you work backward. Total cost divided by months available equals monthly savings requirement. If you need $45,000 in 42 months, that's roughly $1,071 per month. If you need $18,000 in 24 months, that's $750 per month. The math is just division. A calculator can do it.

And here's the crucial part, the part where most advice falls apart because it relies on you being a different person than you actually are: you automate it immediately. Same day you get paid, before you've bought groceries or paid for parking or grabbed drinks with coworkers or done literally anything else with that money, the transfer happens automatically. Completely separate account. Different bank if possible. An account you don't see when you check your balance on your phone at 11 PM wondering if you can afford pizza. An account labeled something that makes it real—"Spain Ceramics Fund" or "Condo Down Payment" or whatever makes the goal feel like an actual place you're traveling toward, not just a number.

This isn't willpower. This is removing the decision entirely. You're not trusting yourself to do the right thing every two weeks for the next three years—you're building a system where the right thing happens whether you feel like it or not.

Let me show you what this looks like in practice, because theory is useless without a real example you can map onto your own life.

Meet Vanessa. She's 34, works in HR for a mid-size tech company in Denver, makes $68,000 a year—about $4,400 monthly after taxes. She's been talking about leaving corporate work and getting a master's in social work for six years. Six years of "someday" and "when I'm more financially stable" and "maybe next year when things calm down." Six years of watching friends make career changes while she stayed put, playing it safe, waiting for the perfect moment that never came.

The degree she wants costs $52,000 total for the two-year program at University of Denver. She wants to start in three years, which gives her 36 months to save. That's $1,444 per month.

When I told her that number, she laughed. Not a happy laugh—a bitter, defeated one, the kind that means *of course, of course it's impossible, why did I even let myself hope?* "Are you serious? I can barely save $200 a month now. You want me to save seven times that?"

But here's what Vanessa was actually doing: she was trying to save from what was left. And what was left, after rent and bills and groceries and gas and her gym membership and Target runs and happy hours and subscription services and occasional online shopping and ordering dinner when she was too tired to cook and life just generally happening—what was left was somewhere between zero and $200, depending on the month. Sometimes less. Sometimes she'd overdraft and not even realize it until the fee hit.

So we tried something different.

We opened a separate savings account at Ally Bank—different from her regular bank, no debit card, transfers take two business days to complete. We labeled it "MSW Program 2029." Not "savings" or "future" or anything vague. The actual goal, right there in the name. And we set up an automatic transfer of $1,444 to hit that account the same day her paycheck deposited. Same day. Before anything else happened.

Then we looked at what remained: $2,956 to cover absolutely everything else for the entire month.

Vanessa's rent was $1,350 for a one-bedroom in a decent neighborhood. Utilities averaged $120—electric, gas, internet. Car payment and insurance: $380. Student loans from undergrad: $290. Phone: $85. That's $2,225 in truly fixed costs, the stuff that doesn't change month to month. Which left $731 for everything else—groceries, gas, going out, entertainment, clothes, random Amazon purchases, all of it.

"That's impossible," she said. And I got it. I really did. $731 sounds impossibly tight when you're used to having $4,400 hit your account and somehow still feeling like there's never enough.

But here's what happened when we actually tracked her spending for a full month—not estimated, not guessed, but wrote down every single purchase. She was spending $520 on food. Let me break that down: $180 on groceries, $340 on restaurants and delivery. Another $180 on subscription services: Netflix, Hulu, Spotify, a meditation app she'd used maybe twice, a meal kit service she kept meaning to cancel, a gym membership to a place she visited twice a month if she was being honest, plus two Patreon subscriptions to podcasts and iCloud storage. Then there was $90 on gas. About $110 on going out for drinks or movies or whatever. And between $150 and $400 on what she called "random stuff"—clothes, skincare, books, things for her apartment, gifts, stuff she saw on Instagram and impulse-bought.

None of it felt excessive in the moment. That's the thing I need you to understand. None of these purchases felt like the reason she couldn't afford graduate school. That's the insidious thing about small purchases—they never *feel* like they're standing between you and your dreams. A $40 dinner doesn't seem like it's preventing you from changing careers. It's just dinner. But $40 three times a week for a year is $6,240. That's twelve percent of her degree. Gone to meals she barely remembered eating a week later.

I'm not saying Vanessa should never eat out. That's not the point, and honestly that kind of extreme deprivation doesn't work anyway—you just crack eventually and binge. The point is she had no idea she was choosing restaurants over graduate school. The decision was invisible. There was no moment where she consciously weighed those two options and picked the pasta.

So we made it visible.

She cut her food delivery from $340 to $120—still eating out twice a week, but being intentional about when restaurant meals actually mattered to her. Birthdays. Dates. Catching up with a friend she hadn't seen in months. Not just Tuesday because she was tired. She canceled the subscriptions she wasn't genuinely using, keeping only Netflix and Spotify, saving $95 per month. She switched to a cheaper gym ten minutes from her apartment, one she'd actually go to because it was convenient, saving another $35. She set a hard budget of $100 per month for "random stuff," and committed to waiting 48 hours before buying anything non-essential.

These changes—none of them that dramatic on their own—freed up about $400 per month. Which meant her actual discretionary spending dropped from $731 to roughly $330 for groceries and essentials. Tight, yes. Impossible? No.

And the savings? Protected. Automated. Happening before she ever saw the money, before she could spend it on something else, before she could talk herself out of it.

Eight months in, Vanessa had $11,552 in her MSW fund.

Let me say that again because I want you to feel the weight of it: for the first time in her adult life, she watched a number grow that represented something she actually wanted, not just something she was trying to avoid. Not debt. Not overdrafts. Not financial disaster. Something she wanted.

And something shifted in how she thought about spending.

She started asking herself a different question when she was about to buy something: *Is this worth delaying school by a week? By two days? By an afternoon?* Because that's what every purchase was now—time. A $30 impulse buy was roughly 5 hours of delayed progress toward her goal. A $150 shopping spree was a full day.

Sometimes the answer was yes. Sometimes she'd have an incredible dinner with friends and think, *Absolutely worth it. I'll remember this.* But most of the time—most of the time—the answer was no. The latte wasn't worth it. The throw blanket wasn't worth it. The slight upgrade in streaming quality wasn't worth it.

Not because she was depriving herself. Because she was finally *choosing*.

(You're probably skeptical right now, and you should be. This sounds like one of those stories that only works for someone who was secretly spending $2,000 a month on nonsense, and you're thinking, *My budget is already tight. I don't have $400 of waste lying around.* Fair. And I'll be honest—for some people, the math just doesn't work without increasing income, which we'll cover extensively in Chapter 6. But before you decide you're that person, actually track your spending for one full month. Not estimate. Not guess. Track. Write down every purchase. You might be surprised. Most people are.)

Now let me break down the actual framework, step by step, so you can apply this to your specific situation. Because this only works if you can actually implement it, not just nod along and close the book.

Step one: Define the goal with painful specificity.

Don't write "save for the future" or "build wealth" or any of that vague aspirational language that sounds good but means nothing. Write exactly what you're saving for, how much it costs, and when you want it. "Save $30,000 for a food truck by December 2028" or "Build a $15,000 emergency fund within 18 months" or "Save $200,000 for retirement by age 50 so I can quit and do pottery full-time."

The more visceral and concrete, the better. If you can visualize it—actually picture yourself signing the lease on the food truck, or getting the call from your boss to quit, or walking into the pottery studio you've been dreaming about—it'll survive contact with temptation. Abstract goals die the second you see a good sale.

Step two: Calculate the monthly savings target.

Total cost divided by number of months. Basic division. If you're saving for retirement or something without a fixed endpoint, use an online calculator—there are dozens of free ones, just search "retirement savings calculator"—to estimate what you need to save monthly based on your timeline and expected returns.

Don't aim for perfection here. A reasonable estimate beats paralysis by analysis. You can adjust later.

Step three: Automate the transfer immediately.

Not next week. Not after you "get your budget in order." Today. Right now, if possible. Set it up to happen on payday, before any other spending occurs. Use a separate account—ideally at a different bank—with a name that reminds you why this matters. Make it slightly inconvenient to access. No debit card. A transfer delay. Something that creates friction between impulse and action.

The key is removing the decision from your future self. Your future self is tired and stressed and wants pizza. Your future self cannot be trusted to consistently do the hard thing. Your current self needs to build a system that protects your future self from themselves.

Step four: Track your actual spending for 30 days.

Not what you think you spend. Not what you hope you spend. What you *actually* spend. Every dollar. Use an app like Mint or YNAB, use a spreadsheet, use a notebook you carry around—doesn't matter. Just capture everything.

This part is annoying. Do it anyway.

Step five: Identify what you can reallocate.

Look for three types of expenses:

Things you don't value at all. Subscriptions you forgot about. Habits you don't even enjoy anymore but keep doing out of inertia. The gym membership you haven't used since February. Those are easy cuts.

Things you value but could do differently. Eating out versus cooking at home. New books versus the library. Premium versions of services versus basic. Brand-name groceries versus store brand. These require thought—you're not eliminating the thing, you're finding a cheaper way to get the same value.

Things you value deeply that are worth keeping. This is important. Some spending is genuinely worth it. Maybe coffee with your best friend every Sunday morning is sacred time that matters more than the $25 it costs. Keep it. This isn't about performing deprivation—it's about aligning spending with actual values.

Step six: Make specific cuts and commit to them for 90 days.

Don't vaguely promise to "spend less on groceries" or "eat out less." Decide exactly what you're doing: "I'm spending $140 on groceries instead of $210 by meal planning every Sunday and shopping with a list." Specificity creates accountability. Vague intentions create nothing.

Commit to 90 days. Long enough to form a habit, short enough that it doesn't feel permanent if you hate it.

Step seven: Revisit quarterly.

Life changes. Goals change. Your income might increase, or an unexpected expense might throw everything off, or you might realize you were too aggressive with the cuts and you're miserable. Review the system every three months to make sure it still fits your life.

This is a living system, not a prison sentence.

Let me be very clear about something, because most budgeting advice completely misses this: this isn't a deprivation framework. I really need you to understand that. Most budgeting advice is built on shame and restriction and white-knuckling your way through every purchase, saying no to everything, hating your life while you save. That approach fails. It always fails. Because humans aren't wired to sustain misery indefinitely. You'll crack eventually, then feel guilty, then decide you're bad at money, then give up entirely.

This is different.

This is about making the invisible visible—seeing the real trade-offs you're already making every day, whether you realize it or not—and then choosing deliberately instead of on autopilot.

Let me give you another example, because I know one story isn't enough to make this feel real and applicable to your specific situation.

James is 29, works in logistics for a distribution company, makes $51,000 a year—about $3,400 monthly after taxes. He's been dreaming about taking a year off to through-hike the Pacific Crest Trail since he read Cheryl Strayed's *Wild* in college. That was seven years ago. He keeps talking about it. Keeps planning it in his head. Keeps not doing it.

The goal: save $25,000 for a year of minimal expenses while hiking—gear, permits, travel to and from the trail, food resupply boxes, and a small cushion for when he gets back and needs to find work and a place to live. Timeline: 30 months. Required savings: $833 per month.

James was spending like this: $950 on rent in a house with two roommates, $100 on utilities, $250 on his car payment, $180 on car insurance, $85 on his phone, $200 on student loans. Fixed costs: $1,765. That left $1,635 for everything else, and he was consistently ending each month with less than $50 in his checking account. Often less than $20.

Where was it going? He genuinely didn't know. So he tracked it, and what he found kind of stunned him.

Turns out: $450 a month on his truck. Not the payment—that was separate. This was gas, modifications, truck accessories, detailing, the occasional repair. He loved his truck. It was his hobby, his identity, the thing he and his buddies bonded over on weekends. Another $280 on eating out and bars—not fancy places, just the default social option. $120 on his gym and a climbing gym membership. $95 on subscriptions—streaming services, Spotify, a gaming service. And between $400 and $600 on what he vaguely categorized as "miscellaneous"—camping gear he didn't need yet, equipment upgrades, clothes, concert tickets, random purchases that seemed small in the moment.

Here's the thing, and this is where I had to be honest with him in a way that felt uncomfortable: James didn't want to give up his truck hobby. And I wasn't going to tell him he had to. But he needed to decide whether his truck was more important than hiking the PCT, because the math said he couldn't fully fund both.

Not without increasing his income or extending his timeline by years.

After sitting with it for a few days—really sitting with it, not just reflexively defending his choices because someone questioned them—he realized something. The truck modifications were mostly social. Keeping up with his friends' builds. Trying to maintain a certain image. Proving something, maybe, about who he was. The actual enjoyment he got from driving it? That didn't require a new intake system or premium detailing every month or the latest accessories.

He cut his truck spending to $150 a month—enough for gas and basic maintenance, nothing extra. He reduced eating out to $120 by cooking more and being selective about which social invitations actually mattered. He kept the climbing gym because that was directly related to preparing for the hike, ditched the regular gym he barely used, saved $45. He gave himself a firm $200 monthly budget for miscellaneous, no exceptions, and started using a 48-hour rule before buying anything non-essential.

That freed up $515 per month. Not quite the $833 he needed, but close.

So he picked up occasional weekend shifts doing inventory work at a warehouse—physical, kind of boring, but it paid decent and he could do it on his own schedule. That brought in an extra $350 per month on average, which he funneled directly into the PCT fund. The entire amount. Not some of it. All of it.

Eighteen months later, James gave his notice. He had $16,400 saved, plus he'd sold his truck (which hurt more than he expected, but also felt like shedding weight he'd been carrying) for another $8,200. More than enough. He started the trail in April 2025 and finished in September.

I talked to him a few months ago. He's back now, working a different job he actually likes more, living more simply, sharing an apartment with one roommate instead of two so he has more space and quiet. And he says—and I believe him—that the six months of hiking were worth every dinner he didn't buy, every truck part he didn't install, every time he said no to something that didn't matter so he could say yes to the one thing that did.

I'm not saying everyone should quit their job and hike for six months. That's not the point. I'm saying: if you have a thing that matters that much—really matters, not just sounds appealing when you read about it or watch a documentary—then treating it like an optional luxury you'll get to "someday" is a choice. A choice to prioritize a thousand small, forgettable things over one big, potentially life-changing thing.

And that's fine, if it's conscious. If you're genuinely happier with the daily pleasures than the distant dream. But most people aren't choosing. They're just drifting. The current is carrying them, and they're telling themselves they'll swim for shore later, when they're stronger, when the conditions are better.

The Fund Your Values system forces the choice into the open.

Here's a simple worksheet structure you can use to build your own version. Grab a piece of paper or open a notes app right now—not later, now—and fill this out:

Your Bigger Life Goal: [Write it specifically. Not "travel more" but "spend three months in Japan." Not "financial security" but "own a house."]

Total Cost: [Actual dollar amount. Research this if you don't know.]

Timeline: [How many months from now?]

Required Monthly Savings: [Total cost ÷ timeline]

Current Monthly Income (after taxes): [Look at your actual paycheck, not your annual salary divided by 12.]

Fixed Costs: [List each one: rent, utilities, car payment, insurance, loans, subscriptions you genuinely can't cut. Add them up.]

Remaining After Fixed Costs: [Income minus fixed costs]

Desired Savings Amount: [Your required monthly savings from above]

What's Left for Everything Else: [Remaining after fixed costs minus desired savings]

Then—and this is critical, this is where most people stop because it's uncomfortable—actually track your spending for 30 days. Write down every purchase. Every coffee, every lunch, every impulse Amazon order. Then compare what you're currently spending in that "everything else" category to what you'd have available after funding your goal.

The gap between those two numbers is what needs to change.

Some people look at that gap and panic. "I'd have to cut my spending by 40%! That's impossible!" And yes, sometimes it's significant. Sometimes it feels insurmountable. But here's what I've watched happen dozens of times, and what I hope will happen for you: when people see the real numbers, laid out clearly, they also see how much they're spending on things that don't actually matter to them.

Subscriptions they forgot about. Habits they don't even enjoy anymore. Purchases made from boredom or anxiety or just because the money was there and why not.

You're not cutting 40% from your happiness. You're cutting 40% from autopilot. From drift. From the accumulated weight of a thousand tiny decisions you never actually made.

And if the gap still seems impossible after eliminating all the waste? After cutting everything that doesn't genuinely matter to you? Then you have three honest options: extend your timeline (save the same amount over more months, which reduces the monthly requirement), reduce the goal's cost (find a cheaper version of the dream, get creative about how to achieve the same underlying desire), or increase your income (which we'll cover extensively in Chapter 6, and which is often more possible than you think).

Those are real options. Not failures. Not admissions of defeat. Just different paths to the same destination. But they only become clear—you can only make an informed choice—once you've done the actual math and faced the real trade-offs.

There's one more piece to this that most budgeting systems completely ignore, and it's maybe the most important part: the emotional weight of visibility.

When you're operating on the pay-what's-left model, your financial situation is always vague. You're "doing okay" or "a little tight this month" or "trying to be better." There's no number attached to your dream. No clear progress. No way to know if you're winning or losing because the game itself is invisible. You can't measure what you're not tracking.

But once you set a specific savings target and start tracking it? You know exactly where you stand at any moment. You can see that you're 23% of the way to your goal. That last month you saved $920 instead of $850 because you got a small bonus and put the whole thing toward the dream. That you're four months ahead of schedule, or two months behind, or right on track. The number becomes real. It has weight and meaning.

That visibility is uncomfortable at first. Really uncomfortable. It forces you to confront whether you're actually prioritizing the thing you claim to care about. Whether your actions match your stated values. Whether the story you tell yourself about who you are and what you want is actually true.

But over time—and I've seen this shift happen in person, watched it change people's relationship with money entirely—it becomes motivating. You start to feel ownership over the number. Pride when it grows. Urgency when it stalls. You check the account balance not out of anxiety but out of genuine excitement to see the progress.

There's a concept in psychology research called implementation intentions—the idea that people are far more likely to follow through on a goal when they've specified exactly when, where, and how they'll act. "I want to exercise more" fails almost every time. "I will go to the gym Monday, Wednesday, and Friday at 6:00 AM before work, and I've already packed my gym bag the night before" succeeds at dramatically higher rates.

Same principle here.

"I want to save for my dream" fails.

"I will automatically transfer $680 to my Dream Business Fund every payday, and I will not reduce that amount unless I lose my job or have a genuine emergency" succeeds.

The Fund Your Values system isn't magic. It won't make money appear that doesn't exist. It won't solve systemic poverty or erase the reality that some people are genuinely struggling to survive, let alone save. But for most people reading this—people who have some income, some ability to make choices about spending, some dream they've been deferring—it will show you whether your life actually reflects your values or whether you've been lying to yourself about what matters.

And once you see that clearly, once the invisible becomes visible, you can't unsee it. You can't go back to pretending the drift is fine, that someday will come on its own, that wanting something is the same as moving toward it.

The question isn't whether you can afford your dream. The question is whether you're willing to choose it, concretely and consistently, over all the small things you're choosing now.

Tom had the categories. What he didn't have was a map of where the money was actually going between paychecks.

Chapter 4: The Flexible Spending Audit

There's a $4.73 charge on my credit card statement from six weeks ago. Starbucks, probably. Maybe Dunkin'. I remember the day - Tuesday, March something - but not the coffee. Not the reason. Not what I was doing there or whether it was worth it.

That's what this chapter is about. Not your rent. Not your car payment. The other stuff. The flexible spending.

Most budgets treat this category like loose change rattling around in a drawer. "Miscellaneous." "Fun money." "Everything else." It's what's left over after the important stuff is handled, and honestly, that's why most budgets fail. Because life doesn't happen in the "important stuff" column. Life happens in the margins. The coffee you grabbed because you were running late. The book you bought because the cover caught your eye. The dinner out because cooking felt impossible that night. None of it feels significant in the moment. By the end of the month, it's hundreds—sometimes thousands—of dollars you can't quite account for.

You know the feeling. You check your balance and think, *Where did it all go?* You weren't reckless. You didn't buy anything crazy. But somehow the money's just... gone.

Here's the thing most budgeting advice gets wrong: they treat discipline as the solution when it's actually part of the problem. They tell you to white-knuckle your way through, to resist every temptation, to treat yourself like you can't be trusted with money. That works for about two weeks. Maybe three if you're stubborn. Then life shows up—a friend's birthday, a busted phone charger, an actual moment of joy you want to participate in—and the whole system collapses.

You don't need more willpower. You need a system flexible enough that life's surprises don't derail you.

But—and I know what you're thinking here—how can you build a flexible system if you don't even know where the money's going? You can't. That's the uncomfortable truth. You're flying blind, making spending decisions based on vibes and vague guilt rather than actual information. It's like trying to navigate with a map that just says "somewhere around here." Doesn't work.

So before we can talk about spending *better*, we need to talk about spending *awareness*.

I spent eighteen months hitting every savings target I set. I had a color-coded spreadsheet—green for groceries, blue for utilities, purple for the emergency fund that I was so proud of building. Every dollar accounted for. Every month I'd transfer the designated amount to savings and feel this little hit of accomplishment. I was *winning* at budgeting.

Then my best friend called. Destination wedding. Costa Rica. She'd met someone who made her laugh so hard she snorted wine out of her nose, and now they were getting married on a beach, and would I please, *please* come?

I opened my spreadsheet. Ran the numbers. Flight, hotel, dress, gift, a few dinners out. I could technically do it—I had the money—but it would mean completely blowing up three months of savings targets. And I'd built this system that was so tight, so perfectly calibrated, that there was no room for... this. For the thing that actually mattered.

I'd optimized myself into a corner.

I went to the wedding (I'm not a monster), but I felt guilty the entire time. Every piña colada felt like a betrayal of my financial goals. I'd built a budget that couldn't bend, and when life asked it to, the whole thing nearly snapped. That's when I realized: the problem wasn't my spending. The problem was that I had no idea which parts of my spending actually brought me joy and which parts were just... habits. Background noise. Money leaving my account because it always had, not because it served any real purpose.

That's what a Flexible Spending Audit fixes.

Let's get practical. The mechanics are straightforward, though they require more honesty than most people are comfortable with. For thirty days—one full month—you're going to track every single discretionary dollar that leaves your possession. Not estimate. Not ballpark. *Track*.

I can hear the groaning from here. "I don't have time for that." "It sounds obsessive." "I already know I spend too much on [coffee/takeout/shoes/insert your personal vice here]."

Maybe. But I'd bet real money you don't actually know the number. You know it's *too much*—whatever that means—but you don't know if it's $50 too much or $500 too much, and that difference matters a lot when you're trying to build a bigger life.

Here's what you need: something to record with. A notes app on your phone works. A small notebook in your pocket works. A spreadsheet works if that's your thing, though don't get precious about it—this isn't about building a beautiful data visualization, it's about capturing information. The tool doesn't matter. Consistency does.

Every time money leaves your account for something that isn't a fixed cost (rent, insurance, loan payments) or a value investment (the categories we built in Chapter 3), you write it down. Date. Amount. What it was for. That's it. Three pieces of information.

And—this is important—you don't change your behavior during the tracking month. Don't suddenly start packing lunch every day if you normally buy it. Don't skip your Friday night drinks with friends because you're embarrassed to log them. The whole point is to see your actual spending patterns, not the idealized version you wish existed. Think of it as a scientist observing their subject. No judgment. Just data.

Thirty days later, you'll have something most people never get: a true picture of where the flexible money goes.

Now comes the interesting part. You're going to categorize everything you tracked. And I mean *everything*, broken down into specific buckets—not vague umbrella terms like "food" or "entertainment."

Here's what I mean. "Food" is useless as a category because it mashes together your weekly grocery run (probably necessary) with the $47 you spent on Thai takeout at 10 p.m. because you were too tired to cook (maybe necessary, maybe just convenient, maybe actively making your life worse if it's happening four times a week). Break it into pieces: Groceries. Coffee shops. Lunch out. Dinner out. Late-night delivery. Convenience store snacks. Each one is its own line item.

Same with entertainment. "Entertainment" could mean a museum membership you use constantly, or three streaming services you forgot you were paying for, or concert tickets to see an artist who changed your life, or $80 at a bar you don't remember because you were already drunk when you got there. These are not equivalent expenses. They don't deserve the same category.

So get specific. Streaming services. Books. Live events. Movies. Hobbies. Gifts. Clothes. Personal care. Subscriptions you forgot about. Impulse purchases. Whatever categories match your actual life. Ten categories. Fifteen. Twenty if that's what it takes. There's no right answer except honest specificity.

Once you've categorized everything, add up the totals for each bucket. This is where people usually have one of two reactions: complete surprise ("I spent *how much* on iced coffee?") or defensive rationalization ("Well, I *need* those daily lattes, they're part of my routine").

Neither reaction is helpful yet. We're still just looking at numbers.

Here's what you're going to do with those numbers.

I call this next part the Value Alignment Check, which sounds corporate and boring, but I haven't come up with a better name yet. (If you think of one, email me. Seriously.)

For each spending category, you're going to assign two numbers. First: how much you spent in that category over the month. You already have that from your tracking. Second: how much that spending actually aligns with the core values you identified back in Chapter 2. Rate it on a scale of 1 to 5.

A 1 means this spending actively works *against* what you care about. A 5 means this spending is so aligned with your values that you'd fight to keep it in your budget even if money got tight. Everything else falls somewhere in between.

Be ruthless here. Don't rate something a 5 just because you enjoy it. Enjoyment is great—I'm very pro-enjoyment—but that's not what we're measuring. We're measuring *alignment*. Does this expense move you toward the bigger life you're trying to build, or is it just pleasant background noise?

Let me show you what this looks like in practice.

Mark is a 34-year-old graphic designer in Portland. He wants to save for a down payment on a house but feels like his money evaporates every month. He tracked everything for thirty days and categorized it like this:

- Coffee and pastries: $150 - Streaming services (Netflix, Hulu, Disney+, HBO Max): $52 - Online shopping—mostly clothes and tech gadgets: $310 - Eating out: $245 - Gym membership: $89 - Concerts and live events: $95 - Books and magazines: $43

Now Mark goes back to his values list from Chapter 2. His top three were: experiences over possessions, personal growth, and building a stable foundation for the future. With those in mind, here's how he rated each category:

- Coffee and pastries: 2/5 (Tastes good, but it's really just a habit. Not bringing him closer to anything important.) - Streaming services: 2/5 (He watches Netflix regularly, but couldn't tell you the last time he opened Hulu or Disney+. HBO he only got for one show that already ended.) - Online shopping: 1/5 (He's honest enough to admit most of this is impulse buying to feel better after a stressful day. The stuff usually sits in the closet.) - Eating out: 4/5 (About half of this is genuine social time with friends—dinners, weekend brunches. The other half is convenience meals he doesn't enjoy. Mixed bag, but the social component is important to him.) - Gym membership: 5/5 (He actually uses it, it makes him feel better, it's health maintenance. Totally aligned.) - Concerts and live events: 5/5 (This is "experiences over possessions" in action. These are memories he'll keep.) - Books and magazines: 4/5 (He reads most of what he buys, learns from it. Supports the "personal growth" value. Could probably use the library more, but this one's pretty solid.)

Now multiply the spending amount by the alignment score for each category. This gives you a weighted total—a rough measure of how effectively your money is supporting what you actually care about.

- Coffee: $150 × 2 = 300 - Streaming: $52 × 2 = 104 - Online shopping: $310 × 1 = 310 - Eating out: $245 × 4 = 980 - Gym: $89 × 5 = 445 - Concerts: $95 × 5 = 475 - Books: $43 × 4 = 172

Total alignment score: 2,786

That number by itself doesn't mean much. It's not like there's a universal "good" alignment score you're trying to hit. But look at the breakdown. Mark is spending $310 a month on online shopping that he rated a 1 out of 5 for alignment. That's a glaring mismatch. Meanwhile, concerts—something he deeply values—are getting less than a third of that budget.

The Value Alignment Check doesn't tell you what to do. It just makes the mismatches visible so you can make an actual choice instead of sleepwalking through your spending.

Mark decided to cut his online shopping budget by two-thirds. Not eliminate it—he's not a monk, and sometimes you do just need a new phone charger or whatever—but bring it down to around $100 a month. He canceled three of his four streaming services (kept Netflix, which he actually uses). That's $270 a month freed up. He put $200 of it straight toward his down payment savings and kept $70 as a small cushion in his flexible spending category.

Small shifts. Not dramatic. But they moved his money from low-alignment spending to high-alignment goals, and he barely felt the loss because he was cutting things that weren't serving him anyway.

You might be thinking: "This sounds like a lot of work just to tell me I spend too much on stuff I don't care about. I could have told you that for free."

Sure. Maybe. But there's a difference between vaguely knowing you waste money and seeing exactly where it goes. One is a guilt-flavored feeling that doesn't lead anywhere. The other is actionable information.

Most people who try to "cut back" on spending do it backward. They pick an arbitrary number ("I'll spend $200 less this month!") and then white-knuckle their way through, saying no to everything until they crack and binge on something stupid just to feel human again. That doesn't work because it's not based on anything real—it's just restriction for restriction's sake.

The Flexible Spending Audit flips that. You're not restricting first and hoping it sticks. You're gathering information first, then making strategic decisions based on what actually matters to you. The cuts don't feel like deprivation because you're not cutting things you love—you're cutting things that were already failing the alignment test.

There's another benefit too, one that surprised me when I first started doing this with my own spending: it makes you a more confident spender on the things that *do* align.

When you know exactly how much you spend on low-value stuff every month, and you reallocate even part of that toward something meaningful, the guilt evaporates. You stop second-guessing every purchase because you're not operating in the dark anymore. You have a plan. You know what you can afford, what matters, and what doesn't. That clarity is worth more than the money you save.

Let me give you one more example, because I think this is where the rubber really meets the road.

Sarah is a 29-year-old middle school teacher in Atlanta. She earns about $3,800 a month after taxes. She feels chronically broke despite living in a rent-controlled apartment and not having car payments. Where's the money going?

She tracked her flexible spending for a month. Here's what she found:

- Groceries: $380 (She was actually surprised this was so reasonable. Thought it would be higher.) - Coffee shops: $86 - Lunch during the school week: $140 (The school cafeteria food is inedible, and she's too exhausted most mornings to pack anything.) - Dinner out / takeout: $190 - Drinks with friends: $75 - Gym membership: $45 (She hasn't been in four months but keeps meaning to go back.) -

Streaming services: $38 - Skincare and makeup: $95 - Clothes: $120 - Books: $52 - Random Amazon purchases: $83 (Stuff she didn't even remember buying until she checked her order history.) - Gifts: $68 (It was a heavy month—two birthdays and a baby shower.)

She did the Value Alignment Check. Sarah's core values from Chapter 2 were: meaningful relationships, creativity, and financial security. Here's how she scored everything:

- Groceries: 5/5 (Basic necessity, but also she enjoys cooking when she has time. Solid.) - Coffee shops: 3/5 (Sometimes it's a social thing, sometimes it's just caffeine. Middle of the road.) - Lunch at work: 2/5 (Pure convenience. She hates it, actually—it's expensive and not even good.) - Dinner out/takeout: 4/5 (A lot of this is social—dinners with friends, her weekly standing date with her sister. High value.) - Drinks with friends: 5/5 (This is "meaningful relationships" in action.) - Gym: 1/5 (She's paying for something she doesn't use and feels bad about. Total misalignment.) - Streaming: 3/5 (She watches some of it, not all of it. Fine but not essential.) - Skincare/makeup: 3/5 (Some of this is self-care she genuinely values, some is impulse buying from TikTok ads.) - Clothes: 2/5 (Mostly impulse purchases that don't fit right and sit in her closet.) - Books: 5/5 (She reads constantly. This is creativity fuel and genuine joy.) - Amazon randomness: 1/5 (Can't even remember half of it. Clear waste.) - Gifts: 5/5 (Relationships matter to her. She likes giving thoughtful gifts. Totally aligned.)

When she calculated the alignment scores, two things jumped out. First: she was spending $120 a month on clothes she didn't love and $83 on Amazon impulse buys she forgot about within days. That's over $200 a month on stuff that scored a 1 or 2. Second: she was spending $140 a month on work lunches she actively resented.

Here's what she changed. She canceled the gym membership (freed up $45). She committed to meal-prepping on Sunday afternoons—not elaborate stuff, just simple lunches she could grab in the morning. That cut her work lunch spending from $140 to maybe $30 in ingredients, saving around $110 a month. She deleted the Amazon app from her phone to remove the friction-free impulse buying, and she gave herself a hard $50 monthly budget for clothes—only for pieces she genuinely loved and would wear immediately.

Those changes freed up about $345 a month. She put $300 of it into a high-yield savings account she'd been wanting to open (financial security value), and she kept $45 as extra cushion in her flexible spending budget for spontaneous plans with friends (meaningful relationships value).

Did her life suddenly transform overnight? No. But she stopped feeling broke. She had breathing room. And the money she *was* spending felt intentional instead of like a slow leak she couldn't control.

One of the patterns I see over and over—and maybe you're already spotting it in these examples—is that the biggest flexible spending drains aren't usually the things we love. They're the things we tolerate. The subscriptions we forgot to cancel. The convenience purchases we make because we're too tired to do it the cheaper way. The stuff we buy out of boredom or stress or because we think we *should* have it, not because we actually want it.

Those are the easiest cuts to make because you're not giving up anything valuable. You're just stopping the leak.

But here's where people get tripped up: they treat the Flexible Spending Audit like a one-time event. They do it once, make some cuts, feel virtuous for a month, and then drift back into old patterns because they never built the underlying awareness into their routine.

This isn't a one-and-done fix. It's a practice. A monthly check-in. (You don't have to track every purchase forever—though some people find they actually like it once it becomes a habit—but you should at least do a spot-check every month or two to make sure you haven't started leaking money in new places.)

Think of it like this: your budget isn't a static document. It's a living system that needs regular maintenance. The Flexible Spending Audit is part of that maintenance. You're not trying to achieve perfect spending and then lock it in forever. You're building the awareness to notice when things drift off-course and the tools to correct them before they become a problem.

Now, I know some of you are still skeptical. You're thinking, "Sure, this works for people who have money to waste on gym memberships they don't use and impulse Amazon purchases, but what about me? I'm already scraping by. There's nothing to cut."

Maybe. But probably not.

I've done this exercise with people at every income level, and the pattern holds: almost everyone has at least some flexible spending that doesn't align with their values. Sometimes it's small—$30 a month on a subscription they forgot about. Sometimes it's significant—$400 a month on stress-relief purchases that don't actually relieve the stress. The dollar amounts vary wildly, but the principle is the same.

And here's the thing: if you're genuinely scraping by, if every dollar is already spoken for and there's no waste to cut, then the Flexible Spending Audit gives you something even more valuable than money to reallocate. It gives you *proof*. Hard evidence that the problem isn't your spending habits—it's your income. And that's a different problem with different solutions, which we'll talk about in Chapter 6.

But most people aren't there. Most people have at least a little room to move things around once they can actually see where the money's going.

So here's your assignment for this chapter. (I'm calling it an assignment because "action step" sounds like something from a corporate training seminar, and I refuse.)

For the next thirty days, track every flexible dollar you spend. Not your rent. Not your car insurance. The other stuff. Coffee, meals, subscriptions, impulse purchases, everything. Use whatever method works for you—app, notebook, spreadsheet, voice memos to yourself, I don't care. Just capture the information.

At the end of the month, categorize everything into specific buckets. Be honest about what you're actually spending on, not what you wish you were spending on.

Then run the Value Alignment Check. For each category, rate how well that spending aligns with your core values (the ones you identified back in Chapter 2) on a 1-to-5 scale. Multiply the spending amount by the alignment score. Look at the results.

You're not trying to hit a specific number. You're just looking for mismatches—places where you're spending significant money on things that score low on alignment. Those are your opportunities.

And then—this is the part people skip—you make one small change. Not ten. Not a complete overhaul of your entire financial life. *One* strategic cut or reallocation based on what you learned. Maybe it's canceling a subscription. Maybe it's meal-prepping to reduce takeout spending. Maybe it's deleting a shopping app from your phone. Whatever it is, make it small enough that it doesn't feel like punishment and specific enough that you'll actually do it.

One change, based on real information about your actual spending patterns and values. That's where momentum starts.

Because here's what nobody tells you about budgeting: the goal isn't to spend less. The goal is to spend *right*. To align your money with what matters so that every dollar is working toward the bigger life you're trying to build instead of just evaporating into the void.

The Flexible Spending Audit is how you figure out which dollars are working and which ones are just along for the ride. And once you know that—once you can actually *see* it instead of just feeling vaguely guilty about it—everything else gets easier.

But seeing where the money goes is only half the equation. The other half is knowing what to do with that information. Which cuts actually move the needle, and which ones just make you miserable without freeing up enough money to matter? That's what we're tackling next.

The $4.73 bought me nothing I can remember. That's the real cost - not the money, but the fact that it disappeared without buying anything worth keeping.

Once you see the leaks, the question becomes: which ones are accidents, and which ones are quietly buying you something you'd miss?

Chapter 5: Strategic Cuts Without Sacrifice

The average American spends 47% of their take-home pay on non-negotiables - rent, utilities, insurance, minimum debt payments - before they've bought a single meal. Which means that for someone making $50,000 after taxes, there's only $26,500 left to cover food, gas, clothing, everything else, and somehow save for a bigger life.

Then one Tuesday afternoon in March, she walked into my office looking like she hadn't slept in a week. Dark circles under her eyes. Hair pulled back in a ponytail that had probably been there since Monday. She sat down in the chair across from my desk, stared at her hands for what felt like a full minute, and finally said, "I can't do this anymore."

Her voice cracked on the word "anymore."

I'd been the one encouraging her to "stay the course." I'd praised her discipline at every session, celebrated her milestones, told her she was doing everything right. And she burned out completely. Two weeks later, she'd racked up $3,000 in new charges. Not because she was irresponsible. Because the dam finally broke and three months of deprivation came flooding out in one long weekend of fuck-it spending.

That failure—and it was *my* failure as much as hers—taught me something I should have known from the start: a budget that doesn't account for burnout isn't actually working. It's just a timer counting down to collapse.

Most budgeting advice treats discipline as the solution. Cut harder. Try harder. Want it more. But discipline isn't the solution—it's often part of the problem. You don't need more willpower. You need a system flexible enough that life's surprises don't derail you, and human enough that you can actually live inside it for longer than three months.

You know how this goes. You start strong. You cancel subscriptions. You meal prep on Sundays. You bring your coffee from home in a travel mug. You skip happy hour. You say no to the office birthday cake. For a few weeks, maybe even a few months, you feel virtuous and in control.

Then your kid gets sick and you're eating hospital vending machine food for three days straight. Or your car breaks down and the repair costs $800 you don't have. Or you just hit a wall—it's Tuesday, you're exhausted, and you cannot face another goddamn homemade salad.

The budget doesn't bend. So you do.

And then you feel like you've failed.

Let me tell you what that actually costs you.

It costs you trust in yourself. Every time you "break" the budget, you internalize a story about your own lack of discipline. You start to believe you're the problem. Not the system that set you up to fail. Not the advice that told you humans can run on willpower indefinitely. You.

I've watched clients carry that story for years. They'll sit across from me and apologize for being "bad with money" when the truth is they're not bad with money—they're just trying to operate a system designed for robots, not humans.

It costs you relationships. When you're operating from scarcity and deprivation, every invitation becomes a minefield. You start declining so often that eventually people stop asking. One day you realize it's been two months since anyone texted you to hang out and you can't tell if it's because they stopped inviting you or because you trained them that the answer would always be no.

It costs you joy. When every purchase is analyzed through the lens of guilt and failure, even the things you *do* spend money on stop feeling good. You take your kid to the movies and spend the whole time calculating what this is costing you instead of watching their face light up at the screen.

And here's the cruelest part: it often doesn't even work. When you finally crack—and you *will* crack, because humans aren't built for indefinite deprivation—you don't just spend a little. You binge. I've seen people "save" $300 over two months of white-knuckle discipline, then blow $800 in a single weekend. The math doesn't math.

So if discipline and deprivation aren't the answer, what is?

Strategic reduction.

The difference isn't semantic. It's foundational. Deprivation is about what you're giving up. Strategic reduction is about what you're choosing instead.

Think about your spending not as individual line items but as trade-offs. Every dollar you put toward one thing is a dollar you're not putting toward something else. The question isn't "Can I afford this latte?" The question is "Do I want this latte more than I want [the thing I'm actually saving for]?"

A guy named David came to me a few years ago. Mid-30s, software engineer, solid income—six figures. He wanted to save for his daughter's college fund. She was seven at the time. He had a decade to build up a real cushion, and he knew he should be socking away $500, maybe $800 a month. But he couldn't seem to do it.

He "knew" he should cut back on eating out. He'd tried. Multiple times. He'd last maybe two weeks and then he'd crack and he'd be back at his favorite restaurant three nights a week, dropping $60 a pop.

We didn't talk about what he needed to give up. We talked about what he wanted to choose.

Turns out, what he actually wanted wasn't some abstract number in a college savings account. What he wanted was the peace of mind of knowing his daughter wouldn't graduate with debt. A specific, visceral image: his daughter at graduation, celebrating instead of calculating loan payments. His daughter saying yes to a job she loved instead of a job that paid enough to cover her monthly bills.

Once he could see that trade-off clearly—not "give up Thai food" but "choose college fund over Thai food three nights a week"—the decision got easier. Not easy. Easier.

He still ate out. But he cut it by more than half because he *wanted* to, not because some budget told him he was bad if he didn't. That was an extra $400 a month toward the college fund. And he didn't feel deprived. He felt like he was building something.

You're probably thinking: sure, that works for someone with a comfortable income and discretionary spending to trim. What if there's nothing left to cut?

Fair question. Sometimes there isn't room. Sometimes the problem isn't your spending, it's your income, and we'll talk about that in the next chapter.

But more often than I'd like to admit, there's room. It's just buried under layers of habit and autopilot spending that doesn't actually serve you.

Let me walk you through how to find it.

Start with what I call the Tiered Spending Audit. You've already categorized your expenses back in Chapter 4—Needs, Wants (Essential), and Wants (Discretionary). Now we're going to add another layer inside that Discretionary category.

Grab your list and for every item in the Discretionary column, ask yourself three questions:

What am I actually getting from this?

Not what you're supposed to get. Not what you thought you'd get when you signed up. What you *actually* get.

That gym membership you haven't used in four months? You're not getting fitness. You're getting guilt. That streaming service you signed up for to watch one show and then forgot about? You're not getting entertainment. You're getting a recurring charge.

Be ruthless here. Not in a deprivation way—in a clarity way.

Is there a lower-cost way to get the same thing?

Notice I'm not asking if there's a way to get it for free. Sometimes cheap alternatives suck and you're just going to end up spending the money anyway, plus the cost of the failed experiment.

But often there's a middle path. You don't have to choose between $80 yoga classes and nothing. There are $20 community center classes. There are free YouTube videos. There are donation-based studios where you pay what you can.

Could I reduce the frequency without losing what I value?

This is the one that unlocks the most savings because it doesn't require you to give anything up entirely. You just recalibrate.

Maybe you love going to concerts. But you're going every other week and honestly, half of them are bands you're only sort of into. What if you went once a month, but only to the shows you're genuinely excited about? You spend less. You enjoy it more.

Let me show you what this looks like in practice.

Sarah came to me two years ago. She's 38, elementary school teacher, makes about $52,000 a year. She wanted to save for a down payment on a cabin in the mountains. She'd been tracking her expenses for two months and felt stuck. She was "already being frugal" and couldn't see where else to cut without making her life miserable.

We went through her Discretionary spending together. Dining out: $280 a month. Entertainment: $140. Online shopping: $260. Subscriptions: $65.

She'd already tried canceling subscriptions. She cut Netflix and the meal kit service. That freed up about $20. Helpful, but nowhere near enough.

The problem wasn't that she was overspending. The problem was that she hadn't connected those small expenses to the bigger thing she wanted. The cabin was an abstraction. The burrito bowl she ordered on Thursday night because she was too tired to cook? That was *right now*. Real. Immediate.

So we made it concrete.

She found a listing for a cabin near where she wanted to buy—a two-bedroom A-frame with a wood stove and a porch that overlooked a meadow. She printed out a photo. Put it on her fridge. Every time she was about to make a discretionary purchase, she'd look at that photo and ask: "Do I want this more than I want to be sitting on that porch?"

Sometimes the answer was yes. And that was fine. This isn't about never spending money on anything fun. It's about making the trade-off visible.

But most of the time? The answer was no.

She loved trying new restaurants. But when we really dug into it, she was honest: half the time, she wasn't even enjoying it. She was just tired and didn't want to cook. It wasn't about the food. It was about the path of least resistance.

So we didn't eliminate dining out. We made it intentional. Once a week, she'd pick a place she was genuinely excited about—her "splurge night"—and she'd go, order whatever she wanted, and enjoy it without guilt. The other nights, she cooked.

That alone cut her dining expenses by about $180 a month.

The online shopping was trickier because it didn't feel like a problem. Just... things. A candle here. A book there. A sweater on sale. But when she added it up—$260 a month—it shocked her.

We implemented a 72-hour rule. Any non-essential purchase over $30 had to wait three days. She'd put it in her cart, close the browser, and come back in 72 hours. If she still wanted it after three days—genuinely wanted it—fine. Buy it.

But most of the time, the urge passed. That cut her online shopping by about $140 a month.

She was already barely using two of her four streaming services—one she'd signed up for to watch a single show eight months ago and forgotten to cancel, another she shared with her ex-boyfriend and hadn't had the heart to ask him to remove her login. Cutting those freed up another $25.

Total: $345 a month. Over $4,000 a year.

She wasn't living like a monk. She was still eating out, still buying things she wanted, still enjoying her life. But she'd shifted from autopilot spending to conscious choice.

She told me a few months later that the weirdest part was that she didn't miss most of what she'd cut. She thought she would. She thought she'd feel deprived. But mostly she just felt... lighter.

Here's what I want you to try.

Pull up your own Discretionary spending—you've already got it categorized from Chapter 4. Pick one category. Just one. Somewhere you suspect there's some autopilot spending happening.

Apply those three questions. What are you actually getting? Is there a cheaper way? Can you reduce frequency without losing what you value?

Don't try to overhaul your entire financial life in one weekend. That's the deprivation trap again, just wearing a different hat. Just pick one category. Make one change. See how it feels.

If it feels like punishment, stop. Reevaluate. You're not doing this to make yourself miserable. You're doing this to fund the life you actually want. If a particular cut isn't serving that goal, it's not strategic. It's just painful. And painful doesn't last.

But if it feels like relief—like you've stopped spending money on something that wasn't really adding value anyway—lean into that. Build on it.

I know what you're thinking: this is all well and good for discretionary spending, but what about the big stuff? Rent. Car payments. Childcare. Student loans. The things that eat up 70% of your income before you even get to the "fun" categories.

You're right to push back on that. Those big fixed expenses are harder to move. Sometimes impossible. I'm not going to sit here and tell you to "just move somewhere cheaper" when you're locked into a lease, or "just sell your car" when you live somewhere with no public transit.

But sometimes those big expenses *can* shift. Not overnight. Not without planning. But over time, with intention, they can become part of your strategic reduction plan.

I had a client, Rebecca, who was spending $1,950 a month on rent for a two-bedroom apartment in a nice part of town. She lived alone. She liked the space. But when we really dug into it, she admitted she mostly used the second bedroom for storage. Expensive storage. Her out-of-season clothes, some boxes she hadn't unpacked from her last move three years ago, a treadmill she'd bought with good intentions and used exactly twice.

She wasn't going to break her lease—that would've cost her two months' rent as a penalty, and that math didn't work. But when it came time to renew, she moved to a one-bedroom in the same neighborhood for $1,500. That's $450 a month. Over $5,000 a year.

The principle is the same whether you're cutting $25 in unused subscriptions or $450 in rent you don't need. Ask what you're actually getting. Ask if there's a different path. Ask if the trade-off serves what you're building toward.

Strategic reduction isn't about living smaller. It's about living more deliberately. It's about choosing what stays and what goes based on what actually matters to you, not what you think you're supposed to want or what looked good when you signed up for it three years ago.

Start with one category. Make one intentional choice. And see where it takes you.

Maria had cut everything cuttable. The gap was still there.

Chapter 6: Boosting Income for Accelerated Savings

There's a moment that happens to almost everyone who gets serious about saving money. You've cut the streaming services. You're meal-prepping on Sundays. You said no to the third round of drinks last Friday, and yes, you felt a little virtuous walking home early.

That's when the math becomes brutally clear: you can't cut your way to the life you want. Not at this pace.

I remember hitting that wall myself about eight years ago. I'd been tracking every dollar, trimming everywhere that seemed reasonable, and I was *proud* of the discipline. But I was trying to save for a down payment on a house, and at the rate I was going, I'd be ready to buy sometime around my fiftieth birthday. The spreadsheet didn't lie. I could shave another twenty bucks off my grocery bill, sure—eat even more rice and beans—but that wasn't going to fundamentally change the timeline. The numbers just didn't add up to the life I wanted, not without something else shifting.

Most money advice stops at the cutting phase. It's all about deprivation, sacrifice, finding waste. And look, that stuff matters—we spent a whole chapter on strategic cuts. But there's a ceiling to how much you can reasonably trim before your life starts feeling smaller instead of bigger. You run out of subscriptions to cancel. You're already cooking at home most nights. What's left? Stop seeing friends entirely? Never leave the house?

The thing nobody talks about enough is the other side of the equation: the top line. Earning more money isn't sexy advice. It doesn't fit on an Instagram infographic. It sounds like "just work harder," which feels dismissive and exhausting. But here's what I've learned—and what changed everything for me and for dozens of people I've worked with since: adding income, even small amounts, creates momentum that cutting alone never does. It's psychologically different. Cutting always feels like loss. Earning feels like possibility.

You're probably skeptical. I would be too. "Sure, just earn more money—why didn't I think of that?" It sounds glib, like telling someone who's depressed to just cheer up. But stay with me here, because I'm not talking about overhauling your entire career or launching some massive business venture. I'm talking about strategic, small-scale income additions that fit around the life you already have. Most people are sitting on at least two or three realistic ways to add a few hundred dollars a month to their income without taking on a second full-time job. They just haven't connected the dots yet.

Let me tell you about Marcus. He worked in IT, decent salary, nothing extravagant. He and his wife were trying to save for their kids' college funds, but progress was glacial. They'd already cut back on eating out, scaled down their vacation budget, all the usual moves. Marcus was handy with computers—obviously, given his job—but he'd never thought of that as something he could monetize outside of work. Then his neighbor mentioned she'd pay someone to set up her new laptop and transfer all her files from the old one. Marcus did it one Saturday afternoon. She handed him $75.

It was a tiny thing. Pocket change in the grand scheme. But it made him realize something: people around him had tech problems all the time, and most of them had no idea how to solve them. He wasn't going to quit his day job and start a full consulting firm, but he *could* help a few neighbors and friends each month. He put up a post on Nextdoor offering basic tech help—setup, troubleshooting, file transfers, that kind of thing. Within two weeks he had four paying clients. He charged $50-75 per job depending on complexity, worked maybe six hours total across a couple of evenings and one Saturday morning. That month he cleared an extra $280.

Not life-changing money. But here's what happened: Marcus and his wife had been saving about $300 a month for college funds through sheer willpower and sacrifice. That $280 nearly *doubled* their monthly contribution. Their progress timeline got cut almost in half. Same level of sacrifice on the cutting side, but now the math actually worked. The psychological shift was even bigger than the financial one. Instead of feeling like they were losing things—giving up restaurant meals, skipping weekend trips—they felt like they were *building* something. Marcus was using a skill he already had, helping people who genuinely appreciated it, and accelerating toward a goal that mattered to him. It didn't feel like deprivation. It felt like momentum.

I know what you're thinking: "I don't have a marketable skill like that."

You probably do, though. You're just not seeing it because you've never thought about it through this lens. Most marketable skills aren't exotic. They're ordinary things you happen to be better at than the average person, or things you already do that other people find difficult or time-consuming.

Think about it this way: what do people ask you for help with? Not at work, necessarily—just in life. Do friends text you when they need advice on what to wear to an interview? Are you the person relatives call when they can't figure out their phone settings? Do you have a knack for organizing spaces, or explaining complicated things in simple terms, or fixing broken furniture? These aren't resume-builders. They're potential income streams.

I met a woman named Priya at a workshop I ran last year. She was a middle school English teacher, worked long hours, felt maxed out on energy. She was convinced she had zero time or skills for a side income. During the brainstorming exercise, someone asked her what she did for fun. She said she loved thrift shopping and had basically furnished her entire apartment from estate sales and secondhand stores. I asked if she was good at it. She laughed and said, "I mean, yeah, I find incredible stuff for nothing."

That's a skill. It doesn't sound like one, because it's fun for her, but most people are terrible at thrift shopping. They don't know where to look, what to look for, how to spot quality, how to negotiate. Priya knew all of that instinctively. I suggested she try flipping furniture—buy underpriced pieces at estate sales, clean them up if needed, resell them on Facebook Marketplace or Craigslist for a profit. She was hesitant. It seemed too simple, maybe too much work.

She tried it anyway. Spent $40 on a solid wood side table at an estate sale one Saturday morning. It had ugly brass hardware and a dated finish, but the bones were good. She swapped the hardware for $12, wiped it down, took decent photos, listed it for $120. It sold in three days. After expenses she'd made $68 profit for maybe two hours of her time—most of which was driving to the sale and meeting the buyer. She did it again the next weekend with a bookshelf. Then a set of chairs. Within two months she had a rhythm: hit estate sales on Saturday mornings, list items by Sunday evening, make deliveries or arrange pickups during the week. She was bringing in an extra $250-400 a month, depending on what she found.

Priya didn't quit her teaching job. She didn't start a furniture restoration business. She just took something she was already doing for fun and added a small profit motive to it. The money went straight into her savings account—she was building an emergency fund that had been stuck at $800 for over a year. Six months later it was past $2,500 and climbing. That's the difference between cutting alone and adding income. Cutting might have gotten her to $1,000 eventually, but it would've taken twice as long and felt like deprivation the whole way.

Here's the part that trips people up, though. Let's say you do start bringing in extra money—a couple hundred bucks a month from freelancing, or selling stuff, or dog-walking, or whatever fits your life. What happens to it? Be honest. For most people, it just... disappears. It gets absorbed into the general spending. Maybe you're a little looser with your grocery budget that week, or you say yes to happy hour because hey, you earned extra this month. The lifestyle expands to meet the income. You worked for that money, and you have nothing to show for it.

This is where most people sabotage themselves without realizing it. They do the hard part—they actually generate the extra income—but they don't do the easy part, which is deciding where it goes *before* it arrives. You need a system. Not willpower, not discipline—a system.

I call it Income Allocation, and it's stupidly simple. Before you earn the first dollar of extra income, you decide what percentage goes directly to your bigger-life goal. Not "I'll save whatever's left." Not "I'll try to put most of it away." A specific percentage, decided in advance, non-negotiable.

Here's how I do it, and how I've seen it work for dozens of other people: pick a number between 50 and 75 percent. That's the portion of any extra income that goes straight to savings before you touch it. If you earn an extra $300 from freelancing and your allocation is 60%, then $180 goes directly into your designated savings account.

The remaining $120 is yours to use however you want—cover the costs associated with earning that income, put toward taxes if needed, or just spend guilt-free as a reward for your effort.

The percentage matters less than the consistency. What you're building is a reflex, a habit, an automatic system. You're not relying on future-you to make a good decision when the money hits your account and you're tempted to use it for something immediate. You've already made the decision. The system executes it for you.

Let me walk you through the mechanics, because this is where theory becomes practice. You need a dedicated savings account—separate from your emergency fund, separate from your regular checking, separate from everything else. This account has one job: hold the money that's going toward your bigger-life goal. Maybe that's a down payment on a house. Maybe it's a dream trip to Japan. Maybe it's paying off your car loan so you can free up that monthly payment for other goals. Whatever it is, this account is the physical representation of that goal.

Open the account. Most banks let you do this online in about ten minutes. Label it something specific—not "Savings 2" but "Italy Fund" or "Debt Freedom" or whatever resonates with your actual goal. Then set up an automatic transfer. This is the critical step. The moment your extra income hits your checking account, a predetermined amount—your allocated percentage—moves automatically to the goal account. You don't manually move it later. You don't wait until the end of the month to see what's left. It happens immediately, without you having to think about it.

This is paying yourself first, but specific to the extra income you're generating. It's creating a firewall between the money and your normal spending patterns. And it works because it removes the decision point. You can't spend money you never see.

I'll give you a real example. My friend Alicia started offering virtual bookkeeping services for small businesses—she'd done accounting at her day job and realized she could do the same thing remotely in the evenings. She brought in about $400 a month starting out. She and her husband were saving for a bigger apartment so their two kids could each have their own room. They decided on a 70% allocation rate. That meant $280 went automatically into their "New Place Fund" on the 1st of every month, right after her invoices cleared.

They didn't have to talk about it. They didn't have to decide each month whether to save the money or spend it. The system made the decision for them. The remaining $120 covered the upgraded internet plan she needed for video calls, the occasional software subscription, and a little cushion for coffee or lunch out as a reward. She didn't feel deprived. The extra work felt worth it because she could see the New Place Fund growing every single month.

Six months in, Alicia got more efficient and started taking on bigger clients. Her income jumped to $700 a month. Because they'd set the allocation as a *percentage* rather than a fixed dollar amount, their savings contribution automatically increased too. 70% of $700 is $490. They didn't have to recalculate anything. The system scaled with the income. After fourteen months of this, they had over $6,000 in that account—enough for the deposit and moving costs on a better apartment. Without the allocation system, I'd bet most of that money would've evaporated into daily life.

Now, I can hear the objection forming. "That's great for them, but what if my income is unpredictable? Some months I make $200 extra, other months nothing." Fair point. The allocation system still works—you just adapt it. On months where you earn extra, the percentage rule kicks in. On months where you don't, you don't stress about it. You're not going backward. And here's the thing: even inconsistent extra income adds up faster than you think. Three months of $200 with a 60% allocation gives you $360 in savings. That's money you didn't have before. It's progress.

The key is separating the act of earning from the act of saving. Earning is variable—it depends on opportunities, time, energy, market conditions. Saving, through allocation, is automatic. You're not trying to will yourself into saving more each month. You're building a system that saves for you.

But let's get practical. You don't have extra income flowing in yet, or maybe you do but it's sporadic and you haven't systematized it. Where do you actually start?

First, you need to identify what you can offer. Not theoretically—practically. This is the brainstorming phase, and it's worth taking twenty minutes to do it properly. Grab a notebook or open a doc on your phone. Make three columns: Skills, Stuff, and Time.

Under Skills, list everything you're legitimately good at. Not expert-level, just competent. Can you edit writing? Design basic graphics? Tutor kids in math? Fix bicycles? Cook really well? Teach someone to use Excel? Organize a cluttered garage? These don't have to be job-skills. They're human-skills, the things you can do that other people struggle with.

Under Stuff, list anything you own that has value but isn't essential to your daily life. Old electronics. Clothes you don't wear. Furniture you don't use. Books, tools, kitchen gadgets, sports equipment. Kids' toys they've outgrown. That treadmill in the basement you haven't touched in two years. Be honest here. If you haven't used it in six months and wouldn't miss it, it goes on the list.

Under Time, estimate how many hours per week you could realistically dedicate to earning extra income without burning out. Be conservative. If you think you have ten hours, write down five. If you think five, write down three. You want this to be sustainable, not a sprint that ends in exhaustion and resentment.

Now look at those three columns and start connecting dots. What's the lowest-effort, highest-return option? Selling stuff is usually the fastest win—it requires no ongoing commitment and generates immediate cash. If you have a pile of things you're not using, list them. Facebook Marketplace, eBay, Poshmark, Craigslist—pick whichever platform fits what you're selling. Take decent photos, price things fairly based on what similar items are selling for, and watch the money come in.

I did this myself a few years back. I had probably fifteen hardcover books I'd read once and never touched again, a bike I'd bought on a whim and barely ridden, and a coffee maker I'd upgraded from. I spent one Sunday afternoon photographing and listing everything. By the end of the week I'd made $240. It wasn't passive income—I had to meet buyers, package items for shipping, answer questions—but it was income I generated from things that were literally collecting dust. That $240 went straight into my house fund.

Selling stuff is finite, though. Eventually you run out of things to sell. Skills-based income is where the real leverage is, because you can keep offering the service month after month. Look back at your Skills column. What's something you could teach, do, or help with that people might pay for?

Here's a test: think about the last time someone asked you for help with something and you did it for free. Could you have charged for that? I'm not saying you should start billing your friends—that's weird—but if your friend needed help and was willing to ask you, there are probably strangers who have the same need and would happily pay.

Take tutoring. If you're decent at any academic subject, you can tutor. High school kids need help with math, science, writing, test prep—always. College students too. Parents are willing to pay $25-50 an hour for someone patient and knowledgeable to help their kid understand algebra. You don't need a teaching degree. You just need to know the subject better than the student and be able to explain it clearly. Platforms like Wyzant and Tutor.com connect tutors with students. You set your rate, your schedule, and work as much or as little as you want.

Or freelancing. If you have any kind of writing, design, administrative, or technical skill, there's demand for it. Upwork, Fiverr, Freelancer—these platforms are filled with people posting jobs that need doing. Data entry, proofreading, basic graphic design, social media management, transcription, virtual assistant work. The pay varies wildly, but you can start small, build a reputation through reviews, and increase your rates as you go. A friend of mine does transcription work a few evenings a week while watching TV. She's fast and accurate, makes about $300 a month, barely thinks of it as work.

Then there are local, physical services. Dog walking. Pet sitting. Lawn mowing. House cleaning. Handyman tasks. Grocery shopping and delivery for elderly neighbors or busy families. These aren't glamorous, but they're consistent and they pay. Apps like Rover, TaskRabbit, and Thumbtack make it easy to find people who need these services. You set your rates, accept the jobs you want, decline the ones you don't.

I know someone—guy named Brian—who started mowing lawns in his neighborhood one summer because he needed to save for an engagement ring. He had a mower, he had Saturday mornings free, and he knew several neighbors paid a lawn service $40-50 per visit. He offered to do it for $35. Within a month he had six regular clients. Four hours of work on Saturday mornings, $210 a week, and he was outside getting exercise instead of sitting at a desk. He did that for six months, saved over $5,000, and bought the ring. Then he stopped because he'd met the goal. The point isn't that you have to mow lawns forever—the point is that opportunities are everywhere if you're willing to look for them and take action.

But here's where people get stuck. They brainstorm, they identify possibilities, and then they don't actually *do* anything. They overthink it. They worry it won't be worth the effort, or that they'll fail, or that people won't want to hire them. They wait for the perfect opportunity instead of starting with a good-enough one.

So let me cut through that paralysis: start small, start now, and give yourself permission to experiment. Pick *one* thing from your brainstorming—the easiest, lowest-risk option—and try it this week. Not next month. This week. List three things on Facebook Marketplace. Sign up for one freelancing platform and create a profile. Offer to walk your neighbor's dog next weekend. Send an email to two friends mentioning you're available for tutoring and ask if they know anyone who needs help.

You're not committing to anything permanent. You're testing. And here's the secret that makes this whole thing work: the first dollar you earn outside your regular job is the hardest. It breaks a mental barrier. You go from "I can't do this" to "I did this." After that, everything gets easier. The second job is easier to find than the first. The third client is easier to land than the second. You build momentum, competence, and confidence. You stop thinking of yourself as someone who can't earn extra money and start thinking of yourself as someone who does.

Now let's talk about what happens once the money starts flowing. You've set up the Income Allocation system—picked your percentage, opened the dedicated account, automated the transfer. You're contributing to your bigger-life goal every month without having to think about it. That's the foundation. But there are a couple of layers that make this even more powerful.

First, build in a small reward for yourself. This is the 10-20% I mentioned earlier that you allocate to guilt-free spending. It's not optional—it's essential. If every dollar of extra income disappears into some distant future goal, you'll burn out. You're working harder than you were before, and that effort deserves to be acknowledged *now*, not just years from now when the goal is met.

Alicia and her husband did this well. They took 10% of her extra bookkeeping income—about $40 a month initially—and used it for a date night. Nothing extravagant, just dinner out somewhere they wouldn't normally go, or tickets to a movie, or a nice bottle of wine to split at home. It made the extra work feel worthwhile in the present tense, not just as a deferred benefit. They weren't sacrificing their current life for a future one. They were enhancing both.

Second, consider reinvesting a portion of your extra income back into the income-generating activity itself. This is especially relevant if your side income has growth potential. Marcus, the IT guy helping neighbors with tech problems, eventually invested in a better toolkit—a portable external hard drive for faster file transfers, some diagnostic software, business cards to hand out. Total cost maybe $150, but it made him more efficient and more professional. His income went from $280 a month to over $500 within a few months because he could take on more complex jobs and handle them faster.

That reinvestment came from the 30% that wasn't allocated to savings—it was part of the operational budget for the side hustle. He wasn't dipping into the college fund to buy tools. The system had already accounted for it.

The third layer is adjusting your allocation percentage over time. This isn't set in stone. If you started at 50% because that felt manageable, and six months later your income has stabilized and the extra work feels easier, consider bumping it to 60%. You're not increasing the effort, just increasing the efficiency. More of each dollar goes toward the goal. Your timeline to achieving it shrinks.

Conversely, if life gets chaotic—you have an unexpected expense, a health issue, a family emergency—it's okay to temporarily reduce the percentage. The system is flexible. The point isn't perfection; it's progress. Even 25% of extra income going to savings is better than zero. The system survives the disruption, and when things stabilize, you bump it back up.

And here's something I don't want you to miss: the psychological compound effect. Yes, the money itself compounds—you're saving more, and if it's in any kind of interest-bearing account, it grows a little on its own. But the bigger compounding is in your mindset. Every month that you earn extra income and successfully allocate it toward your goal, you're reinforcing a new identity. You're becoming someone who doesn't just wait for things to improve. You're someone who makes them improve.

That shift is subtle at first. You might not even notice it. But over time it changes how you see challenges. Instead of "I can't afford that," you start thinking "How could I afford that?" Instead of "I'm stuck," you start thinking "What options do I have?" You move from a scarcity mindset—where you're just trying to protect what little you have—to an abundance mindset, where you believe you can create more.

This isn't motivational fluff. It's a real, observable pattern. People who successfully add even small amounts of extra income to their lives tend to keep finding ways to do it, because they've proven to themselves that it's possible. They see opportunities they would have missed before. They take action faster because they've done it before and know it works.

What does this look like practically for you, right now? You're going to feel resistance. I need to name that because pretending it won't happen sets you up for failure. You'll think of ten reasons why this won't work for you specifically. You'll tell yourself you're too busy, too tired, not skilled enough, not confident enough. You'll worry about what people will think if you start offering services or selling things online.

That resistance is normal. It's your brain trying to protect you from risk and uncertainty. Acknowledge it, then do it anyway—but small. So small that the resistance barely has time to kick in. Don't try to launch a full business this week. Just list one thing for sale. Send one email. Create one profile on one platform.

The goal for this week—not this month, this *week*—is to take the smallest possible step toward generating extra income. Spend thirty minutes on it. That's it. If nothing comes of it, fine. You're out thirty minutes. But if something *does* come of it, if you make even twenty bucks, you've crossed the threshold. You've proven it's real. And next week, you do it again.

By the end of the month, you'll either have extra money flowing in or you'll have learned something valuable about what doesn't work for you—which means you can try something else. Either way, you're further ahead than you were.

And the beautiful part is that none of this requires perfection. You don't need to earn thousands of dollars a month. You don't need to turn this into a second career. Even an extra $200 a month, allocated consistently at 60%, puts $120 toward your goal every single month. That's $1,440 a year. If your bigger-life goal requires $10,000 in savings, you've just shaved years off your timeline compared to cutting expenses alone.

This is the piece most money advice skips right over, and I think it's because it's harder to package into a neat formula. Cutting expenses is simple: cancel this, stop buying that. Boosting income is messier. It requires creativity, effort, trial and error. It asks you to see yourself differently—not as someone who can only reduce costs but as someone who can create value.

That shift is uncomfortable. It's also worth it. Because once you see that you can influence your income, even modestly, you stop feeling trapped by your current financial reality. You're not just managing scarcity anymore. You're building capacity. And capacity—the ability to generate resources when you need them—is what gives you the flexibility to weather life's surprises without your goals falling apart.

That's what the next chapter is about: building a buffer so your system can absorb shocks without collapsing, and doing it without burning yourself out. Because all the extra income in the world won't help if you're too exhausted to enjoy the life you're building toward.

The question most people get stuck on isn't whether to boost their income—it's *how*. Not the mechanics, but the internal permission structure. Because increasing what you earn almost always requires you to do something that feels uncomfortably self-promotional, transactional, or presumptuous. You have to ask for a raise. Or pitch a client. Or put a price on something you made. And if you were raised to believe that talking about money is tacky, or that your worth should be self-evident, or that good work speaks for itself, those steps feel like violations of who you are.

They're not. They're just unfamiliar. And the gap between unfamiliar and impossible is smaller than it feels.

Start with the lowest-friction option available to you. If you're employed, that's usually asking for a raise. Not because it's easy—it's not—but because the infrastructure is already there. You have a relationship with your employer. You're already delivering value. You're just making the case that the value you deliver is worth more than you're currently being paid. That's not greed. It's alignment.

Most people don't ask because they're worried they'll be told no. That's a real risk. But the bigger risk is spending years under-earning because you never tested whether the answer might be yes. If your performance is solid, if you've taken on more responsibility, if the market rate for your role has gone up, you have leverage. Use it. Write down what you've accomplished in the past year. Quantify it where you can. Then schedule a conversation, not as a supplicant, but as someone presenting a business case. You're not asking for a favor. You're correcting a pricing error.

If you're not employed in a traditional role, or if a raise isn't on the table, the next step is selling something. A service, a skill, a product, your time. This is where most people freeze, because now you're not just asking—you're *offering*. And offering means risking rejection in a way that feels more personal. If your employer says no to a raise, you can tell yourself it's about the budget. If a client says no to your pitch, it feels like they're saying no to *you*.

They're not. They're saying no to the offer, at that price, at that moment, in that context. Which means your job is to get better at making offers that are more likely to get a yes. That doesn't mean lowering your price until someone bites. It means understanding what problem you're solving, for whom, and why your solution is worth paying for.

The simplest way to do this is to start with people you already know. Not because it's easier to sell to friends—it's often harder—but because you can test your pitch in a low-stakes environment. If you're a graphic designer, offer to redo someone's website header. If you're good at organizing, offer to help someone declutter their garage. Charge something, even if it's modest. Not to get rich, but to practice the exchange: I do this, you pay me that, we both walk away better off. Once you've done it a few times, it stops feeling like an imposition and starts feeling like a transaction. Which is what it is.

Then raise your prices. Not because you've suddenly become twice as good, but because undercharging is a tax on your future capacity. If you charge $20 an hour for something that takes you two hours, you've made $40. If you charge $50 an hour, you've made $100 for the same work. That extra $60 isn't just money—it's time. Time you can spend finding another client, or learning a new skill, or resting so you don't burn out. Undercharging feels safer because it increases the chances someone will say yes. But it also locks you into a volume game you probably can't win. You can't do infinite hours. You can do higher-value hours.

The other block people hit is skills. Specifically, the belief that they don't have any worth paying for. This is almost never true. What's usually true is that they've spent years doing things for free—at work, at home, for friends—and so they've internalized that those things have no market value. But someone, somewhere, is paying for what you know how to do. The question is whether you're willing to find out who, and what they'll pay.

If you genuinely don't have a skill that's immediately marketable, you can build one. Not over years—over weeks. Pick something people need, that you're capable of learning, and that has a clear path from beginner to competent. Video editing. Copywriting. Bookkeeping. Social media management. You don't have to be the best. You have to be good enough to solve a problem someone has, and willing to do it for a price they'll accept. Then you do it, you get feedback, you get better, and you raise your rates. That's the entire game.

This doesn't mean you quit your job tomorrow to freelance full-time. It means you do one project. Then another. Then another. And if it works, you keep going. If it doesn't, you try something else. The goal isn't to replace your income overnight. It's to prove to yourself that you can generate money outside the system you're currently in. Because once you know that, the system stops feeling like a cage. It's just one option among many.

The last thing worth saying is this: increasing your income isn't a one-time event. It's a skill you build. The first time you ask for a raise, it'll feel awkward. The tenth time, it'll feel routine. The first time you pitch a client, you'll probably fumble. The fiftieth time, you'll close faster. This isn't about talent. It's about repetition. Every time you do it, you get a little better at seeing yourself as someone whose work has value, and who's allowed to claim that value. And that shift—from waiting to be offered what you're worth, to naming it yourself—is the shift that changes everything.

The money was coming in faster now. That's when most people break.

Chapter 7: The 'Buffer' & Avoiding Burnout

My friend Emma lasted exactly nineteen days. Nineteen days of meal-prepped chicken and rice in those depressing little containers that stack in the fridge like a monument to joylessness.

I went to Iceland with Jenna two years later, after I rebuilt my budget around what mattered instead of what tracked cleanly. The northern lights were worth every dollar I'd protected.

Nineteen days of meal-prepped chicken and rice in those depressing little containers that stack in the fridge like a monument to joylessness. Nineteen days of saying no to every coffee invitation, every happy hour, every movie night. She'd even stopped going to her Thursday evening yoga class—the one thing that kept her sane during a chaotic work week—because the $15 drop-in fee felt irresponsible when she was trying to pay down debt.

She was attacking her credit card debt with the kind of intensity people usually reserve for training for an Ironman. Two thousand dollars a month thrown at a $12,000 balance. On paper, the math worked perfectly. Six months of sacrifice and she'd be free. Half a year of living like a financial monk, then she could go back to being human again.

On day twenty, she bought a plane ticket to Austin she couldn't afford.

Not because she needed to go. Not because there was an emergency or some unmissable opportunity. She bought it because her coworker Melissa mentioned she was going for a long weekend, and in that moment—sitting alone in her apartment at 7:30 on a

Friday night, eating meal-prep container number seventy-three while scrolling through Instagram photos of everyone else's actual life—Emma felt something snap.

The deprivation had built up like water behind a dam. And when it broke, it didn't trickle. It flooded.

The ticket. New clothes because she "needed something to wear." Dinners out every night in Austin. Drinks. Brunch. A $90 vintage jacket from some boutique on South Congress that she didn't even particularly like but bought anyway because buying something—anything—felt like finally being allowed to breathe. By the time she got home, she'd undone three months of progress in one weekend. She'd spent almost $1,800. And the worst part wasn't even the money. It was the shame. The feeling that she'd proven she couldn't be trusted with her own financial life.

I know what you're thinking: Emma just lacked discipline. She should have stuck with the plan. If she'd just powered through another five months, she would have been done.

And maybe there's some truth there. But I've seen this exact pattern play out dozens of times now, with people who have way more discipline than Emma, way more than me, probably way more than you. It's never really about willpower. It's about the fundamental misunderstanding most of us have about how sustainable change actually works.

We've been sold this idea that budgeting means becoming a financial monk. That the path to stability requires total renunciation of anything enjoyable until you've "earned" the right to live again. It's the same logic behind crash diets—deprive yourself completely, hit the goal, then return to normal. Except it doesn't work for weight loss, and it doesn't work for money either. We know this. We've lived this.

And yet we keep doing it because the alternative feels like giving up.

The human brain isn't wired for indefinite deprivation. It's wired for reward cycles. When you remove all positive feedback from an activity—when every single day feels like grinding discipline with no payoff, when there's no light at the end of the tunnel because the tunnel is your entire life for the foreseeable future—your brain starts treating that behavior as a threat. Not metaphorically. Literally. Your brain interprets sustained deprivation the same way it interprets starvation or isolation: as something to escape by any means necessary.

That's not a character flaw. That's biology doing exactly what it evolved to do.

So here's the stance I'm going to take in this chapter, and it might feel counterintuitive at first: **The key to reaching your financial goals faster isn't cutting out everything enjoyable. It's deliberately building enjoyment into the system so the system doesn't collapse.**

This is where the Buffer comes in.

The Buffer isn't leftover money you might have at the end of the month if you're "good." It's not fun money you're supposed to feel vaguely guilty about spending. It's a pre-allocated, non-negotiable line item in your budget—right there next to rent and groceries and debt payments—that exists for one specific purpose: to let you be human while you're building toward your bigger life.

Think of it this way. You know how flight attendants tell you to put your own oxygen mask on first before helping others? The Buffer is your oxygen mask. It's what keeps you breathing while you're doing all the other hard work of financial restructuring. Without it, you might make it a few weeks. Maybe even a few months if you're particularly stubborn. But eventually, you're going to pass out. And when you do, the damage is usually worse than if you'd just been breathing normally the whole time.

Let me give you a real example of what this looks like in practice.

I worked with a couple—James and Maria—who came to me after their third failed attempt at aggressive budgeting. They were both in their early thirties, combined income around $95,000 a year, living in a one-bedroom apartment in a city where that income meant they were doing fine but not great. They were trying to save for a house down payment, which in their market meant they needed about $60,000. Every time they'd commit to "getting serious," they'd slash their budget to the bone. No restaurants. No concerts. No impromptu weekend trips to visit Maria's sister three hours away. Just work, home, rice and beans, and a growing spreadsheet that tracked every dollar they weren't spending.

They'd usually make it about six weeks before one of them cracked.

Maria would come home with Thai takeout because she'd had a brutal day at work—the kind where her boss had changed the project requirements for the third time that week—and she couldn't face another night of reheating the same chicken stir-fry they'd been eating for nine days straight. Or James would buy tickets to see his favorite band because they were in town for one night only and he couldn't stand the thought of missing them when the venue was literally four blocks from their apartment. Then the guilt would set in. They'd feel like failures. The whole budget would fall apart because if they were already "off track," what was the point of continuing? They'd spend the next month in a kind of financial fugue state, not tracking anything, not saving anything, just trying to forget they'd failed again.

When we first talked—this was over coffee, which James insisted on paying for even though I'd offered, and I remember noticing how he seemed almost defiant about it, like he was proving he wasn't completely broken—James said something I still think about: "I feel like I'm choosing between having a life now and having a life later. And I don't know how to do both."

That sentence right there. That's the trap. The false binary. The idea that you can't make meaningful progress toward your goals while also enjoying your actual life in the present. It's paralyzing. And worse, it's completely unnecessary.

Here's what we did. We looked at their budget—really looked at it, not just the aspirational version they kept trying to force themselves into—and we carved out $400 a month as their Buffer. Four hundred dollars they could spend on whatever they wanted. No tracking required. No guilt. No second-guessing whether this particular expense was "worth it" or justified. It represented about 5% of their take-home income, maybe closer to 4% depending on the month. Everything else in their budget stayed tight and intentional—they were still saving aggressively, still being mindful about their fixed expenses, still brown-bagging lunch most days—but that $400 was sacred. It was their permission slip to be human.

You might be skeptical right now. I would be. Four hundred dollars a month is $4,800 a year. That's almost 10% of their down payment goal. Couldn't they reach it faster without that expense?

On paper, yes. In reality, absolutely not.

Because before the Buffer, they weren't actually saving consistently. They'd have a great month where they saved $2,000, then a disaster month where they saved nothing and actually went backward. The emotional whiplash of deprivation and guilt was costing them far more than $400 a month in lost momentum and actual overspending. With the Buffer in place, they stopped sabotaging themselves. They stopped having those month-destroying blowouts where they'd spend $800 on a weekend trip they hadn't planned because they just couldn't take it anymore. They actually started making consistent progress for the first time in two years.

Within eighteen months—not the twelve months the aggressive plan promised, but eighteen months of actual sustained effort instead of cycles of crash-and-burn—they had their down payment.

And here's the thing that really struck me when we talked after they'd closed on the house: Maria said the Buffer had been the most important part of the whole system. Not the savings strategy. Not the income optimization we'd done. Not even the clarity around their values, though that mattered too. The $400 a month that gave them permission to grab dinner when they were exhausted. To go to a movie when they needed to decompress. To buy a friend a birthday gift without agonizing over whether $30 was too much.

"It sounds weird," she told me, and I could hear her trying to justify it, trying to make it make sense, "but I think we saved money *because* of the Buffer, not in spite of it."

She's right. And it's not weird at all once you understand the psychology.

The Buffer works because it removes the thing that makes most budgets fail: the constant, grinding negotiation with yourself about whether you're allowed to enjoy your own life. Every time you pass a coffee shop and have to decide if you "should" go in. Every time a friend invites you somewhere and you have to calculate whether it's worth it. Every time you want something small—a book, a nice bottle of wine, a new running shirt because your old one has a hole in it—and you have to adjudicate whether that desire is legitimate or just weakness.

That negotiation is exhausting. It burns through your willpower like a gas-guzzling engine. And by the end of a long day of saying no to yourself, when your willpower tank is empty, that's when you make the impulsive decisions that actually derail your progress. That's when you book the flight to Austin.

The Buffer eliminates the negotiation. The decision is already made. You have this money. You're allowed to spend it. You don't need to justify it to anyone, including yourself. That freedom—that small, specific freedom—is what makes everything else sustainable.

Now, let's talk about how to actually implement this for yourself, because the number isn't going to be the same for everyone. James and Maria's $400 worked for their income level and their lifestyle and their specific tolerance for restriction. Your number might be completely different.

Here's where I'd start: look at the last three months of your actual spending. Not what you wish you'd spent. Not what you think you should have spent. What you actually spent. Don't judge it yet. Don't try to optimize it. Just observe it like you're a scientist studying someone else's behavior.

How much are you currently spending on things that fall outside your strict necessities? I'm talking about coffee shops, restaurants, entertainment, hobbies, spontaneous purchases, gifts, the random stuff that just shows up on your credit card statement. Add it up and find the average across those three months.

Let's say you find you're spending about $600 a month on these things. That's your current baseline. That's what your life apparently costs when you're not restricting yourself.

Now, I'm not going to tell you to cut it to zero—we just spent several pages establishing why that doesn't work. But you probably can reduce it somewhat while still maintaining your quality of life. Maybe you bring that $600 down to $400 or $450. That becomes your starting Buffer. You're giving yourself permission to spend that amount guilt-free, which is still a reduction from where you are now, but it's sustainable because it's not deprivation.

The other approach—the one I actually prefer for most people—is to work from a percentage rather than a dollar amount. Five percent of your take-home income is a good starting point. If you bring home $4,000 a month, that's $200. If you bring home $6,000, that's $300. The percentage scales with your income automatically and adjusts if your earnings change, which means you don't have to rethink the whole system every time you get a raise or switch jobs.

Some of you are already doing mental math and thinking, "Five percent? That seems like a lot when I'm trying to save aggressively." I get it. I really do. When you're in debt or behind on your goals, every dollar feels precious. Deliberately allocating money to "fun" feels irresponsible. It feels like you're not taking your goals seriously.

But here's what I've learned from watching hundreds of people try to budget their way to a bigger life: the ones who succeed aren't the ones who deprive themselves the most in the short term. They're the ones who build sustainable systems that actually last. And sustainability requires accounting for human nature. Your nature. My nature. The fact that we're not spreadsheets that can optimize endlessly without breaking down.

You're a person with emotional needs. With a desire for spontaneity and joy. With a limited supply of willpower that gets depleted throughout the day by every decision you make, every temptation you resist, every time you choose the hard thing over the easy thing. The Buffer acknowledges that reality. It's not indulgent. It's strategic.

Let me tell you what I personally do with my Buffer, because I think the specifics actually matter here. Generic advice is easy. Real numbers are harder.

I allocate about 7% of my income to it—a bit higher than the baseline five percent because I know myself well enough to know that I need more flexibility to feel comfortable. I learned this the hard way. I tried 5% for about three months and found myself constantly bumping up against the limit, constantly doing that mental negotiation I'd been trying to eliminate. So I bumped it to 7% and suddenly everything felt easier. That's the number that works for me. Yours might be different.

I break my Buffer down into three categories, though you don't have to do this. Some people prefer one lump sum. I'm detail-oriented in ways that are probably not healthy, so I like the structure.

First, there's what I call "structured enjoyment"—about $150 a month. This covers things like my climbing gym membership, the occasional nice coffee from the place with the good beans instead of the Keurig at home, a monthly dinner at a restaurant I actually want to go to rather than just the cheapest option. These are planned pleasures. I know they're coming. I budget for them specifically. I never feel guilty about them because they're part of the system.

Second, there's "spontaneous yes"—about $100 a month. This is for the unexpected invitations. The last-minute opportunities. The "hey, want to grab drinks after work?" moments that make life feel like life instead of just an endless march toward future goals. Before I had this category, I'd either say no to everything and feel isolated and resentful, or say yes and feel guilty about the spending. Now I can say yes to the things that matter without derailing my budget or my peace of mind.

Third—and this is the part I'm weirdly proud of because it took me forever to figure out—there's "overflow," about $50 a month. This is money that rolls over if I don't spend it. It accumulates in a separate savings account, and I can use it for bigger one-time expenses that bring me genuine joy but don't fit in the monthly Buffer. Last year I used accumulated overflow to take a pottery class I'd been wanting to try for months. It was $300 for the six-week session, which didn't fit in my monthly Buffer, but because I'd been letting that overflow build for about eight months, I could say yes without disrupting my other goals or feeling like I was cheating.

That structure works for me. Yours might look completely different. Maybe you don't need the spontaneous category because you're more of a planner and you know your social calendar a month in advance. Maybe you need a bigger structured amount because you have an expensive hobby that's core to your identity and cutting it would genuinely make you miserable. Maybe you want to skip the overflow entirely and just have two categories, or one. The framework isn't the point. The principle is.

The principle is this: **Your budget should enable your life, not replace it.**

I'll be honest with you—and this might be more honesty than you wanted, but we're this far in so we might as well commit—when I first started advocating for the Buffer approach, I got pushback. Other financial advisors told me I was being soft. That I was enabling bad behavior. That people needed to learn discipline and sacrifice, and by building in "fun money" I was undermining the entire point of budgeting. There's this deep cultural narrative that suffering is noble. That if you're not in pain, you're not really trying. That the path to anything worthwhile requires misery as proof of commitment.

But I've been doing this long enough now to have seen the results. I've watched the deprivation approach fail over and over and over. I've seen people yo-yo between extreme austerity and extreme overspending, never making real progress, just cycling through shame and hope and shame again. And I've seen people implement the Buffer and suddenly—finally—start to move forward in a way that actually sticks.

There's a concept in psychology called "ego depletion." The idea is that willpower is a finite resource that gets used up throughout the day, like a battery that drains with use. Every time you resist a temptation, every time you force yourself to do something you don't want to do, you're drawing from that reserve. By the end of a long day of saying no to yourself—no to the coffee, no to the lunch out, no to the new book, no to drinks with friends—your willpower is depleted. Empty. And that's when you're most vulnerable to making the impulsive decisions that actually derail your progress.

The Buffer reduces ego depletion. It means you're not spending your entire day resisting. You're not white-knuckling your way through every coffee shop, every happy hour invitation, every moment of wanting something small that would bring you joy. You've already decided—ahead of time, when you were thinking clearly, when you weren't exhausted and depleted—that you're allowed to spend this money. The decision is made. The willpower is preserved for the things that actually matter.

Let me give you another example, because I think this is where the concept really clicks for people.

I know a guy named David—we met through a mutual friend, and he reached out after hearing I worked with people on their budgets—who was trying to pay off about $30,000 in student loans. He made decent money, around $65,000 a year working in marketing for a mid-size company. Not struggling, not rich, just middle of the road. But he was frustrated by how slowly the loan balance was decreasing. He'd been making the standard payments for three years and barely made a dent.

Every financial calculator told him he should be putting at least $1,500 a month toward the debt to knock it out quickly. So that's what he tried to do. He built a budget that allocated $1,500 to loans, kept his fixed expenses, and basically eliminated everything else. His grocery budget was $200 a month. He stopped going out. He stopped dating. He canceled his gym membership and started running outside instead, which would have been fine except he hated running and only did it because it was free.

It lasted three months.

In month four, his car needed an $800 repair—something with the transmission that couldn't wait. And because he'd been running his budget so lean, putting every available dollar toward the loans, he didn't have the cash. He put it on a credit card. Then he felt defeated because he was supposed to be getting out of debt, not adding to it, even though car repairs aren't optional and credit cards exist exactly for this kind of emergency. But the emotional logic didn't care about practicality. He felt like a failure.

The next month he kind of gave up on the aggressive payment plan. He dropped back to the minimum payment. He stopped tracking his spending. He went out to eat whenever he felt like it, which was often because he was exhausted and demoralized. Within two months he'd gained back almost $3,000 in credit card debt that hadn't existed before.

When we redesigned his budget together, we did two things. First, we built in a real emergency fund—$2,000 set aside specifically for those unexpected-but-inevitable expenses like car repairs and medical bills. Money that just sat there, boring and unused, until it was needed. Second, we created a Buffer of $300 a month. His debt payment dropped to $1,000 a month to make room for both.

On paper, this looked like slower progress. Instead of paying off the debt in twenty months at $1,500 a month, we were looking at closer to thirty months at $1,000 a month. David was skeptical. I could see it on his face. We were sitting in a coffee shop—his choice, and he bought his own latte without flinching, which I took as a good sign—and he said, "So I'm just giving up? Accepting it'll take longer?"

"No," I told him. "You're accepting reality. You tried the aggressive plan and it failed. Not because you're weak, but because the plan didn't account for actual life. This plan does."

Here's what actually happened: David made that $1,000 payment every single month without fail for twenty-six months straight. He didn't have any more credit card emergencies because he had the emergency fund sitting there waiting. He didn't burn out and quit because he had the Buffer that let him grab coffee with friends, go on a date without agonizing over the cost, buy a new pair of shoes when his old ones fell apart. And because he was making consistent progress instead of yo-yoing between extremes, he actually paid off the debt in twenty-six months—slower than the aggressive plan promised, but faster than the reality of the aggressive plan ever would have delivered.

Consistency beats intensity. Every single time.

So how do you actually set this up in a way that works? Here's the process I walk people through:

Step one: Calculate the number. Use the 5% rule as a starting point—five percent of your monthly take-home income. If that feels too high and you're getting anxious just thinking about it, start with three percent and increase it later. If it feels too low because you've been particularly restrictive lately and you know you need more breathing room, go up to seven or eight percent for the first few months while you adjust.

Step two: Decide whether to subdivide it. Some people prefer to have one lump sum they can use however they want. Simple. Clean. No categories to track. Others—especially if you're detail-oriented or you like structure—find it helpful to break it into categories like I do. Neither approach is wrong. Pick what matches your personality, not what you think you should do.

Step three: Make it a real line item in your budget. This is critical. When you're doing your monthly budget, the Buffer goes in before you allocate money to your variable goals. It's not "leftover money" that you spend if there happens to be anything remaining. It's a planned expense, just like rent, just like your car payment, just like groceries. You're not asking permission to spend it. You're allocating it deliberately because it serves a purpose.

Step four: Separate the money physically if that helps. Some people keep their Buffer in a different checking account so it doesn't get mixed up with regular spending money. Others actually withdraw it as cash at the beginning of the month. I tried the cash method for a while and found it didn't work for me—I'm too much of a card person, and having cash in my wallet made me nervous—but I have clients who swear by it. The physical separation makes it feel more real and reduces the temptation to raid it for other purposes.

Step five: Review it monthly. At the end of each month, look at how you used your Buffer. Did you spend all of it? None of it? Was it on things that genuinely brought you joy, or were you just filling time because you had money allocated? This isn't about judgment. It's about refinement. You're learning what actually matters to you, what's worth spending on, what you can skip without feeling deprived.

Here's what the review process might reveal: Maybe you're consistently underspending your Buffer by $50 a month. That's useful information. You might be able to reallocate that $50 to debt payoff or savings without feeling any more restricted. Or maybe you're consistently overspending it by $50, and you need to either increase the Buffer or get more intentional about what you're spending it on. Both of those are fine outcomes. The point is to notice the pattern and adjust.

The goal isn't to spend every dollar of your Buffer, by the way. It's to have it available without guilt when you need it. Some months you might use $50 of your $300 Buffer and feel completely satisfied. Other months you might use all $300 and wish you had more. Both of those outcomes are fine as long as the overall pattern is working—as long as you're making progress on your bigger goals without burning out.

There's one more piece to this that I want to address because it comes up constantly: **What counts as a Buffer expense versus a regular budget expense?**

This is where people sometimes get tripped up. They'll create a Buffer and then agonize over whether their morning coffee should come from the grocery budget or the Buffer. Whether the streaming service is a necessity or a luxury. Whether meeting a friend for lunch is a Buffer expense or something else. They spend more mental energy categorizing than they would have spent just making the decision.

Here's my take: if you're spending that much energy categorizing, you're missing the point. The Buffer is meant to reduce mental load, not increase it. I'd rather you have a slightly messy system that you actually use than a perfectly categorized system that makes you anxious every time you open your wallet.

That said, I do think there's value in having some general guidelines, even loose ones. For me, the Buffer is for things that are genuinely discretionary and bring you joy. Your Netflix subscription that you use literally every day? Probably a regular budget item. A spontaneous trip to the bookstore because you had a hard week and wanted to browse? Buffer. Your regular weekly coffee on the way to work that's part of your morning routine? Regular budget. The fancy seasonal latte you get on Saturday while you're reading in the cafe for two hours? Could go either way—pick whichever feels right and don't overthink it.

The key distinction is this: regular budget items are things you do consistently, things that would feel like a real sacrifice to cut, things that are woven into the fabric of your normal life. Buffer items are the spontaneous joys, the occasional treats, the things that make life richer but wouldn't devastate you to skip in any given week.

And if you're still not sure, ask yourself this: "If I spent this money, would I feel guilty about it without the Buffer?" If the answer is yes, it's probably a Buffer expense. If the answer is no, it's probably a regular budget item.

Now I want to come back to Emma, the friend I mentioned at the beginning who made it nineteen days before the dam broke and she booked that flight to Austin.

After her trip derailed her debt payoff plan, she called me. She was frustrated and embarrassed and kept apologizing for "bothering me" with this, which made me want to reach through the phone and shake her because that's exactly the kind of self-punishment that makes the whole cycle worse. She thought she'd proven she didn't have what it takes to get her finances under control. She was already talking about just accepting she'd always be in debt, that some people are good with money and some aren't, and she was clearly one of the aren'ts.

I told her she'd actually proven the opposite. She'd proven exactly why the Buffer matters.

We rebuilt her budget together over the next week. This time we included a $250 monthly Buffer. It meant her debt payoff timeline extended from six months to about ten months. Four extra months. When I told her that, she got quiet. I could hear her doing the math, feeling like she was failing before we'd even started.

"Ten months sounds like forever," she said.

"So did six months," I pointed out. "And you didn't make it three weeks."

She laughed, but it was the kind of laugh that's mostly exhale. "Fair point."

You know what? She actually made it. No blowout trips. No shame spiral. No cycle of restriction and rebellion. Just steady, sustainable progress that let her still feel like herself while she was doing the hard work. She kept going to yoga. She met friends for coffee. She bought herself flowers sometimes because she liked having flowers in her apartment. Small things. Normal things. Things that made the ten months feel like her actual life instead of some holding pattern she had to endure.

When she made that final payment—she texted me a screenshot of the zero balance at 11:47 on a Tuesday night—she called me the next day and said something I think about often: "I thought I needed to punish myself to make progress. Turns out I just needed to stop punishing myself."

The Buffer isn't about lowering your standards or settling for less. It's not about giving up on your goals or deciding you don't have what it takes. It's about understanding that the path to your bigger life isn't a straight line of deprivation. It's a sustainable rhythm of effort and recovery, discipline and joy, sacrifice and reward. It's about building a system that works with your humanity instead of against it.

Because here's the truth nobody tells you when you're starting this journey: you don't need more discipline. You probably have plenty of discipline. What you need is a system that doesn't require you to use all of it, all the time, forever. What you need is a budget that gives you room to breathe.

The Buffer is that room.

And once you have it—once you stop spending all your energy white-knuckling through each day, once you stop negotiating with yourself about every small pleasure, once you build a system that actually accounts for the fact that you're human—something shifts. You stop seeing your budget as this punishing force you have to resist and start seeing it as a tool that serves you. You stop feeling like you're failing every time you enjoy something. You start making real progress. Consistent progress. The kind that actually sticks.

In the next chapter, we're going to talk about what to do with that progress. Because once you've built a sustainable system—one with a Buffer that keeps you breathing, one that works with your life instead of replacing it—you need a way to track where you're going and know when you're actually getting there. That's where most people stumble next. They build the system, they start making progress, and then they lose momentum because they can't see it working. They can't feel the change. The numbers tick up slowly in some account they never look at, and eventually the whole thing starts to feel pointless.

So we need to fix that. We need to build tracking into your system in a way that actually motivates you instead of just creating more work. We need to make progress visible. We need to make it feel real.

That's what's next.

Emma had room to breathe. She still didn't know if she was breathing in the right direction.

Chapter 8: Tracking Progress & Staying Motivated

Open your budgeting app right now. How many days has it been since you last checked it? If the answer is more than a week - or if you felt a spike of guilt just reading that question - you already know what this chapter is about.

I don’t track $4.73 charges anymore. Not because I don’t care about small money, but because I’ve learned the difference between tracking and remembering. The money I spend on what matters, I remember without writing down.

She wasn’t crying. She wasn’t angry. Just exhausted in a way that went deeper than lack of sleep. She’d been crushing her debt payoff plan for eighteen months. Ahead of schedule. Ruthlessly disciplined. Every dollar tracked, every category optimized, every impulse purchase shut down before it had a chance to breathe. The budget was working. The numbers proved it. The debt was shrinking exactly as planned.

“I can’t do this anymore,” she said.

I’d been encouraging her to “stay the course.” I thought discipline was the answer—just keep grinding, the finish line is close. She quit six months before she would’ve paid off the last card. Six months.

That failure—and it was my failure, not just hers—taught me something most financial advisors won’t admit: a budget that doesn’t account for burnout isn’t actually working. You can’t sustain discipline in a vacuum. You need to *see* progress. Not in some vague trust-the-process way, but visually. Viscerally. In a format that reminds you why you’re saying no to the spontaneous weekend trip or the nicer apartment or the daily latte that actually makes your commute bearable.

Rebecca couldn't see how close she was. The spreadsheet told her the debt was shrinking, sure, but it didn't tell her she was six months out. It didn't give her a countdown. It didn't show her the finish line getting closer in a way that felt real. And without that visibility, every sacrifice just felt like sacrifice—no payoff in sight, just an endless slog of saying no.

Here's what happens when you don't track properly.

You save money. You cut back. You make the "responsible" choice over and over and over. After three months—maybe six, maybe a year—you look at your account balance and think, *Is that it?* The number doesn't feel different enough to justify all that sacrifice. You can't remember what the starting point was. You have no sense of momentum. So you stop. Not dramatically. You don't blow the whole budget in one weekend bender. You just drift. A little more here. A little less saved there. The bigger life goal fades back into "someday" territory, and you're right back where you started, except now you're also quietly bitter about all that effort that apparently led nowhere.

The cost isn't just the money you didn't save.

It's the dream you shelved. It's the growing suspicion that you're not actually capable of change. It's the resignation that sets in when you've tried the responsible thing and it didn't *feel* like it worked, so why bother next time? You start telling yourself stories: "I'm just not good with money." "Some people can do this, but I can't." "Maybe I'm not meant to have the bigger life."

None of that is true. But without tracking that shows you the distance traveled—not just your current location—it *feels* true.

You might be thinking, "I already track. I check my bank balance every week."

That's not tracking. That's glancing at a number with no context. Real tracking is measuring progress against a destination. It's knowing that six months ago you had $2,000 toward the cabin down payment and now you have $8,500, which means you're 17% of the way there and on pace to hit your goal in four years instead of five. *That's* the difference between staying motivated and quietly giving up.

Let me be clear: this doesn't require complicated software or hours spent poring over spreadsheets. In fact, overly complex systems are almost always the first thing people abandon. I've seen beautiful, elaborate budget trackers with pivot tables and conditional formatting and automated alerts—unused after two weeks because they required a degree in Excel just to update.

The core idea is almost offensively simple. Track your savings against your goal. Make that tracking visible. Actually look at it.

There are two main tools, and I'm going to be annoyingly practical about both: a spreadsheet or an app.

A spreadsheet—Google Sheets, Excel, even a Numbers doc if you're in the Apple ecosystem—gives you complete control. You decide what data to include, how it's displayed, what gets bolded or color-coded or hidden. You can tweak formulas as your goals shift. The downside? You have to manually update it. Every week or month, you sit down and do the thing. No automation. No shortcut. For some people, that manual entry is grounding—it forces you to engage with the numbers, to actually *feel* the progress. For others, it's friction they don't need, one more task on an already overwhelming list.

An app—YNAB, Mint, PocketGuard, EveryDollar, any of the dozen others—offers convenience. Often pulls transaction data directly from your bank. The upside is obvious: less manual work, pretty visualizations, automatic categorization. The downside? You're trusting the app to categorize correctly. If you've ever watched an algorithm confidently label your rent payment as "entertainment," you know that requires supervision. Also, some of these apps cost money, which is ironic when you're trying to save it.

There's no objectively "better" choice. It comes down to whether you value control or convenience, whether you're motivated by the ritual of manual entry or annoyed by it. Either works. What doesn't work is not choosing at all.

Let me show you what this looks like in practice.

Mark—saving for the cabin, remember him?—went with a spreadsheet because he's already comfortable tweaking his budget manually and didn't want to link his bank accounts to yet another service. He created a painfully simple table with four columns: "Goal," "Target Amount," "Saved So Far," and "% Complete."

Under "Goal," he listed: - Cabin Down Payment - Concert Fund - Emergency Buffer

Next to each, the target amounts: $50,000 for the cabin, $2,400 for concerts (his per-year budget for live music, which he'd decided was non-negotiable after realizing it's one of the few things that genuinely recharges him), and $10,000 for the emergency buffer.

The "Saved So Far" column he updates once a month—just types in the current balance for each goal. And "% Complete"? A simple formula: (Saved So Far ÷ Target Amount) × 100. Nothing fancy. He doesn't even have conditional formatting. Just a percentage that ticks up every month.

Except here's what happened that he didn't expect.

He started checking it *between* updates. Not to change anything—just to look. To remind himself that the cabin fund was at 14%, that the concert fund hit 100% and rolled over into next year's allotment, that the emergency buffer was sitting at a comfortable 73% and didn't need aggressive contributions anymore. Those numbers became landmarks. Proof of distance traveled. The percentage climbing from 11% to 14% felt like movement in a way that seeing his savings account go from $5,230 to $7,140 never had.

Sarah, on the other hand, went with an app.

She's a 32-year-old middle school teacher saving for a down payment on a small vineyard in Sonoma County—a long-held dream of leaving her classroom job and running her own tasting room and small-batch production. Her "bigger life" isn't retirement. It's autonomy. Working with her hands. Building something that's entirely hers, where the success or failure is on her, not on whether the district decides to cut her program or whether standardized test scores go up.

She used YNAB because a friend recommended it and because she liked the goal-tracking feature that shows progress bars for each savings target. She set up three goals: - Vineyard Down Payment: $80,000 - Equipment Fund (for a used tractor, crush pad setup, basic fermentation tanks): $20,000 - Transition Buffer (to cover living expenses while she gets the vineyard established): $30,000

The app updates automatically as she moves money into each designated savings category. She can see, at a glance, exactly where she stands. This month she saved $500 toward the down payment, $150 into equipment, and $200 into the transition buffer.

Looking at that breakdown, she realized something. She's falling behind on the equipment fund. She wants to buy that used tractor within two years, and at $150/month she's not going to get there. The goal tracker made that immediately obvious in a way that just checking her savings account balance never would have. She could see the gap between where she was and where she needed to be, and more importantly, she could see *why*—she'd been prioritizing the down payment over everything else without realizing the equipment fund was quietly starving.

But tracking the big goals is only half of it.

You also need to track your *monthly* progress within each budget category, because that's where you catch the drift before it becomes a disaster. Before overspending in "Dining Out" turns into a $400 monthly habit you don't even notice until your savings rate tanks.

Here's a framework I use with almost every client, and it's designed to take no more than fifteen minutes a month: **The Monthly Progress Check-In**. Three questions, answered honestly, with actual consequences.

First: What did I save this month toward my bigger life goals?

Not the total. Break it down by goal. $200 to the cabin and $50 to the concert fund is *different* than $250 total savings, because it tells you whether you're actually funding the things you said mattered or just shoveling money into a generic "savings" account that never gets allocated to anything specific. Generic savings is where money goes to die. It sits there, vaguely accumulating, never attached to a purpose, and eventually you spend it on something you can't even remember two months later because it didn't matter.

Second: Where did I overspend, and why?

Notice I'm not asking *if* you overspent. You did. Everyone does. I do. The question is where and, more importantly, *why*. Was it an unexpected expense—car repair, medical bill, something genuinely unforeseeable? Was it a moment of weakness, the kind we all have where you just don't care about the budget because you're tired and life is hard? Or is this a category that's consistently underestimated, which means your budget is wrong and needs to be adjusted?

That last one is critical. If you overspend on groceries every single month by roughly the same amount, that's not a discipline problem. That's a budgeting problem. Your grocery estimate is too low. Fix the budget, not yourself.

Third: What adjustment can I make next month to stay on track?

This is where you do what Mark did—shift funds, trim discretionary spending, or find a way to increase income. Not as punishment. As calibration. You're not a failure because you overspent. You're a person gathering data and making informed adjustments.

Let me show you how Sarah used this.

Her check-in this month revealed she overspent in "Dining Out" by $100. Not a catastrophic amount, but when she looked closer, she noticed a pattern: she tends to eat out when she's stressed about grading papers. Lunch with colleagues becomes an escape valve. It wasn't really about the food—it was about avoiding the stack of essays waiting in her bag, the knowledge that she'd have to spend her evening slogging through poorly argued paragraphs about symbolism in *To Kill a Mockingbird*.

So her adjustment wasn't "stop eating out."

It was addressing the actual problem: she scheduled dedicated grading blocks on weekends, front-loading the work so it didn't loom over her weekdays. That reduced the stress, which reduced the temptation to escape, which saved roughly $75–100 a month. She transferred that directly to the equipment fund, addressing the shortfall she'd identified earlier.

This is what I mean when I say tracking isn't just about numbers. It's about connecting those numbers to behavior, to values, to the actual texture of your life. Sarah wasn't just tracking dollars—she was noticing that her spending patterns revealed stress she hadn't been addressing. The budget became diagnostic.

And—this is important—tracking also helps you acknowledge setbacks without spiraling.

Because setbacks *will* happen. Unexpected expenses. A month where income dips. A moment of total failure where you just… spend the money anyway, budget be damned, because you're human and discipline has limits and sometimes you need the thing more than you need the goal.

I know what you're thinking: "If I'm going to mess up anyway, what's the point of tracking?"

The point is that without tracking, a setback feels like proof that you're bad at this. That budgeting doesn't work for you. That you might as well give up because clearly you don't have what it takes. *With* tracking, a setback is just data. You can see exactly what happened, how much it cost, and—crucially—that it didn't erase all your prior progress. You're still 14% of the way to the cabin down payment even after the $800 car repair. The concert fund still hit its target even though you went over budget in March. You didn't fail. You hit a bump, and the system absorbed it.

That's the difference between shame and adjustment. One makes you quit. The other makes you recalibrate.

Now let's talk about staying motivated when progress feels slow, because this is where most people quietly give up even when the system is working.

You need milestones.

Not just the big goal—the $60,000 cabin down payment, the $80,000 vineyard, the $25,000 career-transition fund—but smaller markers along the way that give you a dopamine hit *now* instead of three years from now.

Here's why: your brain releases dopamine not when you *achieve* a large goal but when you make *progress* toward it. Every time you hit a milestone—$5,000 saved, $10,000 saved, 20% of the way there—you get a neurochemical reward that reinforces the behavior. It's the same reason video games are so addictive. They don't make you wait until level 100 to feel accomplished. They give you a little win every few minutes. Ding—you leveled up. Ding—you unlocked a new weapon. Ding—you completed a quest. Your brain lights up, and you keep playing.

So take that $60,000 cabin goal and break it into sixty milestones of $1,000 each.

Suddenly it's not an abstract future—it's a concrete present action. Find a way to save $1,000 this month. Then do it again next month. Each time you hit it, you get the satisfaction of progress, which makes it easier to keep going. The goal stops being "someday I'll have $60,000" and starts being "this month I'm going to hit milestone #7."

Sarah and Mark—different Sarah and Mark, a couple saving for the cabin together—used a whiteboard in their kitchen. Divided it into sixty squares, one for each $1,000. Every month, when they hit the target, they colored in a square with a blue dry-erase marker. It wasn't fancy. It was a whiteboard they bought at Target and a marker. But it was *visible*—a constant reminder that they were actually moving, that the goal wasn't static, that every month of saying no to things they didn't really want was getting them closer to the thing they *did* want.

The first few months felt like barely making a dent. Sixty squares is a lot of squares. But as more filled in—five squares, then ten, then fifteen—the momentum became real. Visible. They'd walk past that whiteboard every morning while making coffee, and instead of feeling overwhelmed by how much was left, they'd feel a quiet pride at how many squares were already filled.

Ben took it even further.

He's a 36-year-old software engineer who wanted to leave his job and freelance as a photographer. His bigger life meant building up six months of living expenses—$25,000—so he could take the leap without immediately panicking about rent.

He set a quarterly goal: $6,250 every three months. Then broke that into monthly targets of roughly $2,083. Then broke *that* down by category: $800 from cutting dining out and entertainment, $700 from negotiating lower rates on subscriptions and utilities, and $583 from automating transfers to a high-yield savings account he'd opened specifically for this.

That level of detail wasn't micromanagement. It was creating a clear pathway to the goal so that "save $2,083 this month" didn't feel overwhelming—it felt like three distinct, achievable actions. He knew exactly where the money was coming from. There was no mystery, no vague hope that it would work out. Just a plan.

And here's what happened that he didn't expect: he started to enjoy it.

Not in a masochistic, deprivation-is-virtuous way. But because every month he could see *exactly* what worked. He'd cut $800 from dining out by meal-prepping on Sundays—big batches of chili, stir-fry, roasted vegetables that he could grab throughout the week. He'd saved $700 by calling his internet provider and threatening to switch (they immediately offered him a retention discount he didn't even know existed). The $583 automated transfer happened whether he thought about it or not, pulling the money out of his checking account before he had a chance to spend it.

Progress became predictable. And predictability, it turns out, is incredibly motivating when you're used to feeling like your financial life is chaos you're barely managing.

But what about when you stumble? When life throws an expensive curveball and you miss a milestone?

Ben hit this in month four. Unexpected dental work: $1,200. Crown replacement. He didn't have dental insurance that covered it. He had to pull from his emergency fund, which meant he only saved $883 that month instead of $2,083. He was $1,200 behind schedule.

Here's what he *didn't* do: beat himself up, decide he was bad at this, quietly abandon the whole plan.

Here's what he *did* do: he looked at why he missed the target (unexpected but necessary expense—he wasn't going to walk around with a broken tooth), adjusted his timeline (he'd hit his $25,000 goal in seven months instead of six), and kept going. The tracking showed him that even with the setback, he was still *way* ahead of where he'd been four months ago. He'd saved over $8,000. The milestone system didn't make him feel like a failure—it gave him perspective. He could see the gap, yes, but he could also see all the progress that the gap hadn't erased.

That's the feedback loop: track progress, analyze the results, adjust your strategy, repeat.

It's not linear. You'll have good months and garbage months. Months where everything goes right and you save twice your target. Months where the car breaks down and the cat needs emergency surgery and your kid needs braces and you save nothing at all. The difference is that with tracking, you'll *know* which is which, and you'll know what to do about it. You won't spiral. You'll adjust.

Let me give you a system you can implement this week—not next month, not when things calm down, *this week*—called **The Weekly Financial Snapshot**. It takes fifteen minutes. You don't need new software. You don't need to reorganize your entire financial life. You just need to show up, consistently, and pay attention.

Every week—pick a day, same day every week, set a recurring calendar reminder—you do three things:

1. Review Transactions

Scan your recent transactions. Not every single one. Just look for anything unexpected, anything that feels off, any category where you're clearly overspending. If you see a $47 charge to a streaming service you forgot you signed up for, cancel it now. If you notice you've bought coffee out four times this week and it's only Wednesday, adjust. You're not judging yourself. You're noticing patterns.

2. Update Savings Tracker

Add whatever you saved this week toward each bigger life goal. Update your spreadsheet, your app, your whiteboard, whatever system you're using. This isn't about the amount—it could be $20, could be $200—it's about the *ritual* of recording progress. It keeps the goal visible. It keeps you engaged. It reminds you that the bigger life is still the plan.

3. One Category Check-In

Pick *one* budget category to review in detail. Just one. Ask yourself: Am I on track here? Do I need to adjust for next week? Rotate through categories weekly. This week it's groceries. Next week it's transportation. The week after that, entertainment. You're not trying to micromanage everything at once—you're building familiarity with your spending patterns so nothing surprises you at the end of the month.

That's it. Fifteen minutes.

You're not doing forensic accounting. You're staying connected to your money in a way that's sustainable, that doesn't feel like punishment, that actually gives you information you can use.

I'll be honest: the first few weeks feel awkward. You'll forget. You'll skip a week and feel guilty. That's fine. Just start again. The habit builds slowly, but once it's there, it becomes automatic—less of a chore, more of a quick check-in that actually makes you feel *more* in control, not less.

And control, it turns out, is what most of us are actually craving. Not restriction. Not deprivation. Just the sense that we're steering, that our financial life isn't something that happens *to* us while we watch helplessly from the sidelines.

But even with consistent tracking, even with milestones, you're going to hit stretches where motivation tanks. Where the goal still feels impossibly far away and you're tired of saying no.

This is where visualization matters.

And I don't mean vision boards or manifestation nonsense. I mean creating a physical, tangible representation of progress that you see *every day* without having to open an app or log in anywhere.

Sarah—different Sarah, a graphic designer saving for a year-long sabbatical to travel Southeast Asia and learn ceramics—had the best version of this I've ever seen. She taped a large sheet of kraft paper to her kitchen wall. Across the top, in bright markers: "Sabbatical Fund: Operation Freedom!" Below that, a grid. Months across the horizontal axis, dollar amounts up the vertical. Every month she hit her savings target, she filled in one square with green marker. Different shades of green to show incremental progress—lime green for months she just barely hit the target, dark forest green for months she blew past it.

The genius part? At the bottom, she'd written her estimated departure date. Based on her current saving rate, she'd calculated exactly when she could realistically quit her job and book the flight. Seeing that date get closer—May 2027, then April 2027, then March 2027 as she saved faster than expected—was more motivating than any number in a spreadsheet.

It wasn't about accumulating money. It was counting down to freedom.

Mark adapted this for his workshop fund. He wanted to build a small woodworking shop behind his house—just enough space to escape, build furniture with his hands, rediscover a part of himself he'd lost in the daily grind of his accounting job.

He estimated $8,000 total. Broke it down into $333/month for two years. Used a whiteboard in his garage, divided into twenty-four squares (one per month), and marked each $333 contribution. Under that, a countdown to his estimated start date.

The first few months felt like barely making a dent. But as more squares filled in, the momentum became real. Visible. He'd walk past that whiteboard every time he pulled into the garage, and instead of feeling overwhelmed by how much was left, he'd feel a quiet pride at how many squares were already filled. Sometimes he'd just stand there for a minute, looking at it, imagining the shop he was going to build. The workbench. The tools hung on pegboard. The smell of sawdust. The first project he'd make—a simple cutting board, maybe, just to break in the space.

You don't need kraft paper or a whiteboard. Use a jar filled with marbles—one marble per $100 saved. Use a printout of a thermometer-style tracker taped to your fridge. Use a spreadsheet with conditional formatting that turns cells green as you hit targets. The method doesn't matter. What matters is that it's *visible*, that you don't have to seek it out, that it's just *there* reminding you what you're building toward.

And here's the thing nobody tells you about tracking progress: it doesn't just keep you motivated. It changes the way you think about sacrifice.

When you can see the progress—when the whiteboard squares fill in, when the percentage ticks up, when the jar of marbles gets heavier—saying no stops feeling like deprivation. It starts feeling like momentum. You're not giving something up. You're trading it for something better. The decision to skip the expensive dinner out isn't "I can't afford this." It's "I'm choosing the cabin." The decision to cancel the subscription you barely use isn't "I have to cut back." It's "I'm choosing the vineyard."

That shift—from sacrifice to choice—is what makes this sustainable.

Rebecca didn't have that. She had a spreadsheet that told her the debt was shrinking, but it didn't tell her how close she was to being free of it. It didn't show her the finish line. Every month felt the same: restrict, save, pay down debt, repeat. No sense of progress. No countdown. Just an endless grind with no visible end.

If I could go back, I'd make her break that final $18,000 of debt into eighteen milestones of $1,000 each. I'd have her put a whiteboard on her fridge with eighteen squares, one for each payment. I'd have her write the date she'd be debt-free at the bottom—six months out—and cross off the days. I'd make the progress *visible* so she could see herself getting closer, so every month of discipline felt like momentum instead of punishment.

She might've made it. Or maybe she still would've burned out—burnout is real, and sometimes the answer is to slow down, not to track better. But at least she would've known how close she was. At least the decision to quit would've been informed, not just exhaustion mistaken for failure.

That's what tracking gives you. Information. Perspective. The ability to make decisions based on reality instead of how you feel in the moment. And in a financial life that often feels chaotic and out of control, that matters more than almost anything else.

So here's what you're going to do this week.

Pick your tracking method. Spreadsheet or app—doesn't matter which. Set it up. Add your bigger life goals, your target amounts, your current progress. Break the big goal into milestones. Make it visible. Put it somewhere you'll see it every day.

Then, every week, do the fifteen-minute snapshot. Review transactions. Update your tracker. Check in on one category.

That's it. You're not overhauling your entire financial life. You're just paying attention in a way that's structured enough to catch problems early and celebrate progress often.

And next month, when you look at that tracker and see the percentage climb or the squares fill in or the jar get heavier, you'll feel something shift. The bigger life will stop being a vague someday dream and start being a specific, measurable destination you're actively moving toward.

Which brings us to the question nobody wants to ask: what happens when tracking reveals you're *not* making progress? When the numbers show you're stuck, or worse, moving backward? That's when the system you've built—the flexible budget, the buffer, the tracking itself—either holds you up or falls apart. And whether it holds depends entirely on what we talk about next.

Rebecca could track sustainably now. What she couldn't do was track automatically.

Chapter 9: Putting It All Together: The 'Future Fund' System

The budgets that work aren't the ones you think about most. They're the ones you think about least. Not because they're neglected, but because they've been designed to run without you.

Rachel's daughter is twelve now. She quit dance three years ago, but Rachel kept the recital photo on her desk - not because the costume was expensive, but because it was the moment she realized that 'expensive' and 'valuable' aren't the same thing.

The problem isn't the spreadsheet. The problem is that most budgeting advice treats discipline as the solution when it's actually part of the problem. We're told to white-knuckle our way through temptation, to "just say no" to impulse purchases, to track every penny with the vigilance of an accountant during tax season. And when that inevitably fails—because of course it fails, we're human beings, not robots—we blame ourselves for lacking willpower.

But here's what nobody talks about: the cost of that approach isn't just the money you don't save. It's the slow accumulation of guilt every time you "mess up." It's the bigger life that stays perpetually out of reach because your financial system is built on restriction rather than intention. It's the quiet erosion of hope that happens when, month after month, you're working hard but going nowhere.

I watched this happen to my sister. She'd been trying to save for a down payment on a house for three years. Three years. She had a decent income, no major debt, and she genuinely wanted this. But every month played out the same way: she'd get paid, cover her bills, promise herself she'd save "whatever's left over"—and by the end of the month, there was never anything left over. Not because she was reckless. Because she had no system. The down payment was always the last priority, the thing she'd get to after everything else. And there was always something else.

The last time we talked about it, she said something that stuck with me: "I feel like I'm working so hard just to stay in place."

That's the real cost. Not just the missed opportunity to buy a house. The feeling that your effort doesn't translate into progress. That you're running on a treadmill while everyone else seems to be moving forward.

So where do we actually start putting this all together? Not with another elaborate spreadsheet. Not with another promise to "do better this month." With something concrete you can launch today, a system that doesn't rely on superhuman discipline because it doesn't need to. That's the Future Fund.

Think of it less as a budget line item and more as a dedicated savings vehicle with one specific job: move you toward the bigger life you actually want. Not someday. Now. The core idea is simple enough that you can implement it before you finish reading this chapter: before anything else gets allocated each month, a fixed percentage goes directly into your Future Fund. This isn't your emergency fund (though you should have one of those too). This isn't for car repairs or medical bills. This is exclusively for the things you're actively building towards—the down payment, the career change, the sabbatical, whatever "bigger life" means to you.

I know what you're thinking. "Great, another place my money needs to go. I'm already stretched thin." Fair. But here's the thing: you're going to spend your money either way. The question is whether you spend it intentionally, on things that move you toward the life you want, or whether you spend it reactively, on things that happen to cross your path. Most people are doing the latter and wondering why they never get anywhere.

The first step is honest assessment, and I mean genuinely honest—the kind that makes you uncomfortable. Grab your last three months of bank statements. Don't estimate, don't guess from memory, actually look at the statements. Then catalog where your money went. All of it. Coffee runs, streaming subscriptions you forgot you had, the "I deserve this" purchases after a hard day, dinners out, impulse buys that seemed like good ideas at the time. Add it all up.

Don't judge it. Not yet. Just observe. You're looking for two things: patterns you weren't aware of, and pockets of potential—places where you could realistically divert even a small amount without feeling deprived.

When I did this exercise myself (and yes, I still do it periodically because I'm not immune to lifestyle creep), I found $340 a month going to things I genuinely didn't care about. Not luxuries I loved and consciously chose. Just... stuff. A gym membership I used twice. Food delivery when I had groceries in the fridge. Apps I'd downloaded during free trials and never canceled. None of it was individually significant, but together it was $340 a month—$4,080 a year—that could have been going toward something that actually mattered to me.

That's the awareness part. Now comes the percentage.

A common starting point is 10%—solid, achievable for many people, meaningful enough to create real progress. But don't treat this like a commandment handed down from the budgeting gods. Adjust it based on your current situation and the urgency of your goal. If you're aggressively saving for something with a deadline—a down payment with a specific purchase window, a course that starts in six months—bumping that up to 15% or even 20% might be feasible and will dramatically accelerate your timeline.

On the flip side, if you're just starting out, if you're genuinely financially stretched, if the idea of 10% makes your stomach clench with anxiety—start with 5%. Or 3%. The number matters less than the consistency. A small, reliable contribution every month is far more valuable than a large, sporadic one. You're building a habit as much as building savings.

Here's where most budget advice falls apart: it assumes willpower. It assumes you'll manually transfer money to savings each month, that you'll resist the temptation to skip a month when something comes up. You won't. Or you will for a while, and then you won't. So we're not doing that.

Once you've landed on a percentage, automate it. I'm serious. Set up an automatic transfer from your checking account to a dedicated savings account—labeled something specific like "Down Payment Fund" or "Sabbatical Year" or whatever your goal is—the day after each paycheck hits. Most banks let you schedule this in about three minutes through their app. Do it now. Not later. Now.

This removes the decision from the equation. You don't have to remember, you don't have to muster willpower, you don't have to weigh whether this month is a good month to save or not. It just happens. You treat it like any other essential bill—rent, utilities, insurance—something that must be paid each month. Because it is essential. It's a payment to your future self.

Let me tell you about Sarah. She's thirty-two, works as a marketing assistant, and wants to open her own small bakery. Has wanted to for years. She's good at baking—really good, the kind where friends request specific items for parties and offer to pay. But she's been stuck in the wanting stage because the gap between "I want this" and "I'm doing this" felt impossibly wide.

When she started tracking her spending, she found she was averaging around $300 a month on non-essentials. Mostly dining out (ironic, given she wants to work in food) and impulse purchases—the kind you make when you're tired and scrolling your phone. She decided to start with 10% of her $4,000 monthly take-home pay, which came to $400.

She set up an automatic transfer of $400 from her checking to a separate savings account labeled "Bakery Dreams" every payday. Her initial goal: $5,000 for professional baking classes and basic equipment. She broke that down into milestones: $500 by the end of the first month, $1,200 by the end of month two, $2,000 by month three. Small enough to feel achievable, specific enough to track.

Her celebration triggers? A new cookbook when she hit $500. A weekend baking workshop once she reached $1,500. A fancy stand mixer—the kind she'd been coveting for years—at $3,000. She also told her sister about the goal, which meant someone else was checking in, asking how it was going, keeping it real and present rather than abstract and distant.

Here's what made it work: Sarah wasn't just blindly saving. Each month, she reviewed her progress against her overall budget. If she splurged on something unexpected one week—and she did, because life happens—she consciously looked for ways to trim spending elsewhere to stay on track with her Future Fund contribution. Maybe that meant packing lunch instead of buying it for a few days. Maybe it meant skipping a night out and opting for a movie at home instead. Not deprivation. Conscious choice. There's a difference.

And Sarah's approach wasn't static. When she got a small raise four months in, she increased her Future Fund contribution to $450. When she found a cheaper car insurance rate, the $30 monthly savings went straight to the bakery fund. The goal was to continually accelerate progress, not coast on the initial plan.

This is a living system. It adapts. Because life happens—we've established this. Unexpected expenses arise. Your car needs repairs. Your kid needs braces. You might need to temporarily drop your Future Fund percentage to 5% or even pause it for a month. And that's okay. The difference between this approach and the scattered hope-for-leftovers approach is that this is a conscious decision, a temporary adjustment to a system you'll return to, not an abandonment of the whole project.

But—and this is important—you always prioritize getting back on track as soon as possible. Treat it like a non-negotiable commitment to yourself and your future. Not in a punishing, guilt-laden way. In a "this matters to me" way.

Now let's get more granular, because the Future Fund is the vehicle but you still need to know where you're driving.

Grab a piece of paper or open a new note on your phone. List everything you dream of doing, having, or becoming. Everything. Don't judge, don't edit, don't worry about whether it's "realistic" yet. Just brain-dump. Travel to Japan. Start a podcast. Buy a cabin in the woods. Take a year off to write a novel. Learn woodworking. Go back to school. Whatever. Get it all out.

Then—and this is the hard part—brutally prioritize. Rank those items into three tiers: "Must Haves," "Want To Haves," and "Someday Maybes." Be honest with yourself. This isn't about what should be important, what your parents or partner or society thinks should matter. It's about what genuinely matters to you, right now, in this season of your life. This tiering will guide where your money actually goes.

Next, calculate the savings goal and timeline for those "Must Have" items. Let's say you identified three: a down payment on a small house ($30,000), funding a career change program ($15,000), and taking a three-month sabbatical ($12,000). That's $57,000 total. If you want to achieve all three within seven years, you need to save about $8,143 per year—roughly $679 per month.

I know. That number probably just made your stomach drop. But breaking it down makes it less overwhelming and lets you see exactly what kind of commitment is necessary. You might look at that and realize seven years feels too long—maybe you bump up the monthly amount and do it in five. Or you might realize $679 a month isn't realistic right now, so you extend the timeline to ten years, dropping the monthly requirement to $475. The timeline is negotiable. The specificity isn't. Always have a defined endpoint.

Now for the mechanics. Take your net monthly income—what actually lands in your bank account after taxes and other withholdings. Subtract all your non-negotiable expenses: rent or mortgage, utilities, transportation, groceries, minimum debt payments, insurance. What's left? That's your "flexible" income, the money you have to work with for everything else.

And a big chunk of that flexible income needs to be earmarked for your Future Fund.

Here's where the spending diary comes in, and I know this sounds tedious but bear with me. For one full month—yes, the entire month—track every single penny you spend. There are apps for this (I like Mint or YNAB, though even a simple spreadsheet works). But sometimes pen and paper offers more visceral awareness. Don't change your habits yet. Just observe them.

At the end of the month, categorize those expenses beyond the obvious fixed costs. Look for patterns in discretionary spending. How much went to convenience (takeout, delivery, grab-and-go meals)? How much to subscriptions (streaming, apps, memberships)? How much to impulse purchases? How much to "I deserve this" spending after hard days?

Then compare that spending to your prioritized values list. Are you spending money on things that genuinely contribute to your "Must Haves" or even your "Want To Haves"? Or are you spending it on things that just... happened?

This is where tiered reductions come in. Start with the easiest cuts—subscriptions you don't use, recurring expenses you forgot about, obvious waste. Then move to slightly tougher choices. Maybe you can reduce how often you eat out, find cheaper alternatives for everyday items, downgrade a service you're not fully utilizing.

But here's the crucial part, and this is where most restrictive budgets fail: don't eliminate all joy. You need a "fun money" buffer—a fixed amount each month that you can spend on anything without guilt, without tracking, without justification. For some people that's $50. For others it's $300. It depends on your income and your priorities. But it needs to exist, because a system that demands perfection is a system that will break. You're a human being, not an accounting algorithm. (I can't tell you how many times I've had to remind myself of this.)

Let's go back to Sarah for a second. After cutting back on non-essential expenses—canceling two streaming services she rarely used, meal-prepping on Sundays to reduce takeout, shopping her car insurance and finding a better rate—she freed up an additional $150 per month. Combined with her initial $400 allocation, she was now saving $550 toward the bakery fund. But she also kept $100 as fun money—money she could spend on whatever without tracking it or feeling guilty. Sometimes it went to a nice dinner out. Sometimes to a new plant for her apartment. Sometimes it just accumulated and she'd splurge on something bigger. The point was flexibility, breathing room, sustainability.

What if you're consistently falling short? What if even after trimming expenses, the gap between what you can save and what you need to save feels insurmountable?

This is where additional income comes in, and I know you might be rolling your eyes right now—"Great, just make more money, thanks for the advice"—but hear me out. I'm not talking about getting a second full-time job or sacrificing all your free time. I'm talking about small, strategic side income based on skills or interests you already have.

What do you know how to do that other people would pay for? Tutoring. Freelance writing. Graphic design. Consulting in your industry. Dog walking. House sitting. Photography. Crafting. Baking (like Sarah, who started offering mini dessert boxes to coworkers and friends, earning an extra $150-200 a month). The options are more varied than you think, and even a small additional stream—$100, $200, $300 a month—can significantly accelerate your timeline.

This doesn't have to be forever. It's strategic and temporary, a tool to close the gap between where you are and where you want to be. Sarah's dessert boxes aren't a lifelong commitment. They're a stepping stone to her bakery fund, a way to both make extra money and test market demand for her products. Win-win.

The final piece, and this is the thing that transforms the Future Fund from a static plan into a dynamic system: regularly review and adjust. Life happens. Priorities shift. Your income changes. Unexpected expenses arise. Your budget isn't set in stone—it's a living document that needs to be revisited and refined.

Schedule a monthly "Future Fund check-in." Literally put it on your calendar. Thirty minutes on the last Sunday of the month, or the first Saturday, or whenever works for you. Review your progress. Look at what you spent versus what you planned to spend. Identify any challenges. Make necessary adjustments.

Did you overspend on fun money? Why? Was it a one-time thing or a pattern? Can you find additional areas for savings elsewhere? Did you underspend in some categories—maybe you can reallocate those funds to your Future Fund? Is your side hustle still generating the income you expected, or has it dried up?

This isn't about perfection. It's about conscious choices and consistent effort. It's about staying proactive so you remain on track toward the bigger life you're building.

To make this less abstract, I've created a printable worksheet that walks you through the entire Future Fund setup. You can download it from my website (link in the resources section), but the structure is simple enough that you could recreate it yourself right now.

The first section asks you to list your bigger-life goals. Everything you brainstormed earlier. Next to each goal, estimate its approximate cost. Be realistic, but don't be afraid to dream big. If you're unsure, spend fifteen minutes researching online—what do similar experiences or purchases actually cost? You want a rough idea, not a precise quote.

Then comes the milestone breakdown, which is where abstract dreams become concrete steps. Take your first bigger-life goal—let's say "Take a three-month sabbatical to hike the Pacific Crest Trail"—and break it down.

Phase One might be "Save $8,000 for trail gear and initial travel." Timeline: 10 months.

Phase Two: "Save $15,000 for living expenses while not working." Timeline: another 18 months.

Phase Three: "Negotiate leave with employer or line up freelance work for return." Timeline: 3 months before departure.

Each phase has a specific cost, a specific timeline. Suddenly it's not a distant fantasy. It's a series of achievable objectives.

The heart of the worksheet is allocation. List your current income sources—salary, side hustle earnings, whatever's coming in. Then allocate percentages or fixed amounts to different categories: essentials, debt repayment, emergency fund, Future Fund, fun money. The key isn't rigid restriction. It's intentionality. How much of your income should be directed toward your bigger-life goals based on your priorities and timeline?

Then comes the tracking section. Each month, record what you actually spent in each category versus what you allocated. This isn't about punishment. It's about identifying patterns. Did you consistently underspend on fun money? Maybe you can reallocate some of that to your Future Fund. Did you blow past your grocery budget three months in a row? Time to figure out why—are you impulse shopping when hungry, ordering delivery too often, buying ingredients for recipes you never make?

The worksheet also includes a notes section for reflection. What did you learn this month? What surprised you? What obstacles came up? What worked well? This transforms budgeting from a mechanical task into a tool for self-awareness.

And every three to six months, you revisit the goals themselves. Do they still align with your values and priorities? Life changes. What felt urgent last year might not resonate now. Maybe you thought you wanted to buy a house, but after renting in a few different neighborhoods you've realized you value mobility over ownership. Maybe the sabbatical dream has shifted into a desire for a more sustainable work-life balance in your current job. That's fine. The Future Fund isn't about rigidly adhering to a plan you set once and never reconsidered. It's about creating a financial framework flexible enough to support you as you grow and change.

Sarah's now seven months into her Future Fund. She's saved $3,850 toward her bakery goal—not quite on her original pace because she had to pause contributions for a month when her cat needed emergency surgery, but she's back on track now. More importantly, she told me something recently that stuck with me: "I feel like I'm finally building something, not just surviving month to month."

That's what the Future Fund is really about. Not just the money. The shift from reactive to intentional, from scattered hope to systematic progress. From working hard and going nowhere to working hard and actually moving forward.

You've done the Values Audit. You've identified what truly matters. You've learned to track spending, make strategic cuts, find additional income if needed. Now you're taking all of that and channeling it into one focused system that compounds over time. Not someday when you have more willpower or a higher income or fewer obligations. Now, with what you have, where you are.

The question is what you'll do with that system once it's built—how you'll maintain momentum when the initial excitement fades, when life gets complicated, when the bigger life you're building still feels frustratingly far away. But that's exactly where we're headed next.

Also in the Series

Every book in Money Reset stands on its own — read them in any order. If this one was useful, the library continues:

Tax Strategies to Keep What You Earn

Salary Negotiation Before You Sign

Budgeting for People Who Hate Budgeting

Budgeting From Zero

Budgeting on an Irregular Income

Couples Budgeting

Budgeting After Debt

Budgeting for the Broke Paycheck

Budgeting Without a Spreadsheet

Budgeting for Impulse Spending